östberg™

Sustainometrics

Sustainometrics

W. Cecil Steward

Sharon Kuska

ISBN: 978-0-9846136-5-6

Östberg Library of Design Management
Greenway Communications, LLC, a division of The Greenway Group
25 Technology Parkway South, Suite 101
Norcross, GA 30092
(800) 726-8603

www.greenway.us

First Printing

Cover design: Austin Cramer and Diane Wanek
Layout: K.Designs

Table of Contents

Acknowledgements

A hallmark of any viable effort toward sustainability is the active engagement of a team of talented individuals and the contributions by many people to a common goal. This publication exemplifies those characteristics, both in conceptual constructs and in the practical realization of its final form and content. There are many individuals in our shared networks of associates, organizations, students, colleagues, and friends—regionally, nationally, and internationally—who should be recognized for their contributions to helping this project become a reality. We want to say thank you for all the specific as well as silent contributions from those who have known about or been engaged with us in this work toward sustainometrics.

And we must recognize the following individuals explicitly for their significant contributions along the path of our learning and communications for sustainability: Christine Hunt, graduate assistant in the University of Nebraska College of Journalism, for her research and writing on the subject of consumer consumption; April Kick, graduate assistant in the University of Nebraska College of Architecture, for her research, project assistance with case studies, and skill with computer graphics and graphic communications; ArchRival, a Lincoln-based firm of superior design talent, for its contributions to the EcoSTEP images and the basic analog and electronic renditions of the graphic measurements tool; Diane Wanek, director of communications for the Joslyn Institute for Sustainable Communities, for her graphic design talent, attention to the details of print and media communications throughout the projects, and work of the JISC, which has been formative and constructive to all of our concepts and ideas about community sustainability; Katie Torpy, projects director and administrative manager for JISC, for her reading, critique, and carrying of the load of organizational management for so many of the base-line events in the transformational work of JISC; David Ochsner for his presence and partnership in the genesis case studies and conceptual projects that formed the foundation for the JISC body of work and for his reading, critique, and communications talent during the evolution of the manuscript; Nicholas You, assistant to the director, U.N. Habitat Program, for his inclusion of JISC in the global efforts to bring sustainable values and programs to the world's cities; Mary Ferdig, founder and president of the Omaha-based nonprofit Sustainability Leadership Institute, who has taught us and so many others how the human event of leadership with explicit goals for sustainability must change if community sustainability is our ultimate goal; Jay Leighter, assistant professor at Creighton University, who has given us new tools, principals, and attitudes about community communications for the achievement of sustainable visions of community futures; Jane Gaboury of Greenway Group for her skilled, compassionate, and thorough editing services; and James Cramer, founder and CEO of the Atlanta-based Greenway Group, for his friendship, professional encouragement, wise counsel, sustainability programming, and access to the Östberg Press for the final realization of this publication.

And, finally, it would likely be assumed without comment but explicit acknowledgement is essential to recognize that neither our collaboration nor these networks of engagement and interaction would have been possible without the support and encouragement of the Kuska and Steward families as the journey began and moved through projects and experiences. Thank you for your patience and perseverance!

W. Cecil Steward
Sharon B. Kuska

Prologue

To understand sustainometrics, it is necessary to begin with the original definition of *sustainability* and its three pillars of information—environmental, social, and economic. Together, these pillars were intended to describe how contemporary human life on this planet is and would be ever more interconnected.[1]

We will present an expansion of the original three domains of sustainability into the *five domains* of sustainability: environmental, sociocultural, technological, economic, and public policy. In addition, we introduce the proprietary service-marked EcoSTEP[SM] assessment tool that can be applied at any scale of design, planning, or sustainability problem-solving in public administration. The EcoSTEP[SM] process assists the designer, planner, developer, facility manager, manufacturer, contractor, or public or private administrator in determining decision points, key indicators of potential sustainability, and relative weight or distance from balance that each domain may present in its interdependent state.

The content of this book has three goals:

- Assist the reader in understanding the need to consider five domains of sustainability (in lieu of the original three pillars of sustainability) and their interdependence and interaction upon each other.

- Distinguish the differences between linear reductionist thinking and the thought process of holistic, interdependent, and interactive analyses for optimal sustainable outcomes.

- Demonstrate the use of the sustainometrics tool EcoSTEP^{SM} metrics for direct application to desired design and planning outcomes (or other sustainability intentions in the built environment) through a range of models, indicators, and project scales and applications.

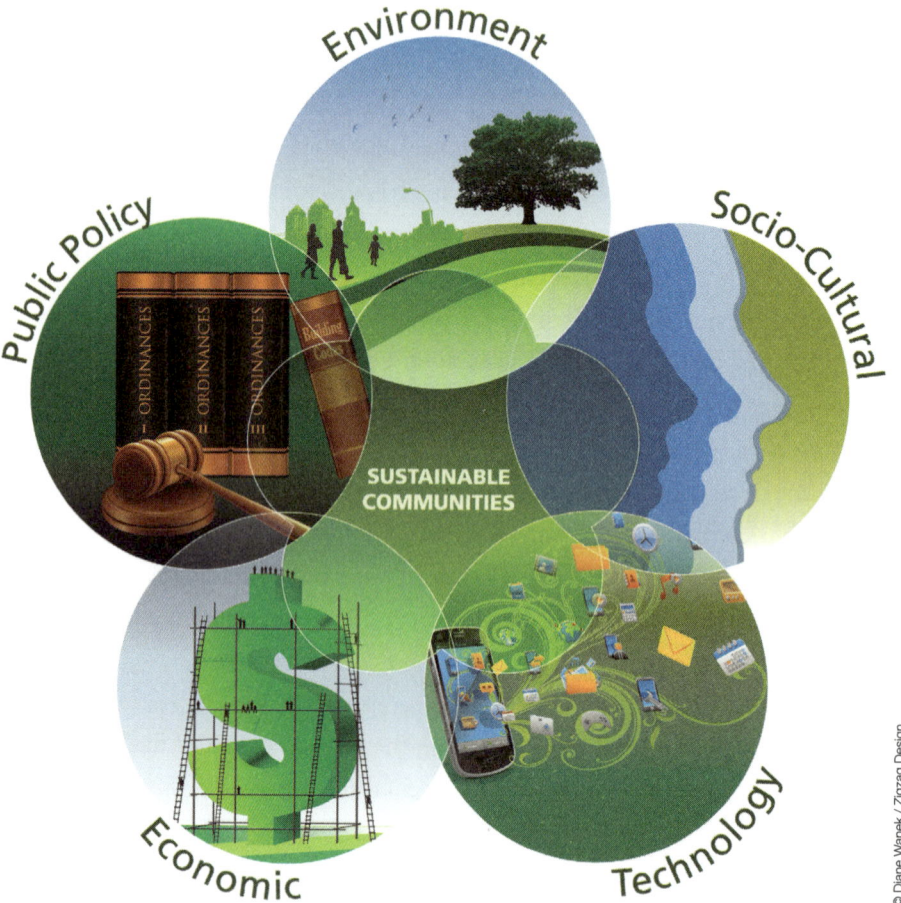

Five Domains of Sustainability[2]

- The **environmental domain** includes assessment of impacts, natural resources, and systems limits of use; emphasis on regional and micro variations in environmental conditions; and the range of impacts on each of the other four domains.

- The **socio-cultural domain** involves reading the culture for distinctions and patterns; understanding historical and contemporary values and trends; the cultural enhancement characteristics of sustainable development; the essential indicators of social and cultural community health; consideration of social and environmental equities; community ethics; and the range of impacts on each of the other four domains.

- The **technological domain** encompasses history; current applications and future uses; emphasis on design and planning with appropriate technologies; technologies and products that can be manufactured from renewable or recycled resources; technologies that influence the sustainability of buildings and communities; life cycle costs, availability, and impacts of technologies; and the range of impacts on each of the other four domains.

- The **economic domain** combines initial costs compared with life cycle costs; cost-benefit characteristics of sustainable development; natural and social capital costs in the world of global free market capitalism; challenges to the planned obsolescence foundation of contemporary economics; public and private capital investment strategies in sustainable development; and the range of impacts on each of the other four domains.

■ The **public policy domain** includes the influence on planning and designing for long-term sustainability; the control of limited resources for a common good; balancing economic, socio-cultural, and technological demands with a carrying capacity of the natural systems; public policies to protect fragile natural resources and eco-systems; public policies and cross-jurisdictional impacts at the community, county, state, regional, and national levels; and the range of impacts on each of the other four domains.

The domains are considered collectively, interactively, and interdependently. This format for a map of any element of a community's use of materials and resources avoids the pitfalls of singular, linear thinking that often results in exclusionary actions and unintended consequences. Using this five-domain map, any development project—be it a building, street of residences, commercial district, neighborhood, community, city, or region—can be planned and described over time to be moving either toward or away from conditions of long-term sustainability. In the mapping and planning process, the challenge for designers, planners, developers, and administrators is to define the appropriate measures of sustainable conditions for the unique community context given the particular project.

The rationale and community-based experiences of defining appropriate sustainability indicators for each of the five domains is described in the following pages. The overall principles and the task of measuring indicators of priorities and progress among and between these five domains can be defined as *sustainometrics*—a holistic system of metrics for sustainability of the built environment.

CHAPTER I

Sustainometrics[3]

T he classic definition of sustainability, paraphrased as appropriating the Earth's resources in a manner that will not prohibit future generations of human inhabitants from meeting their own needs has stood the test of time for a common definition since the last decade of the 20th century.[4] Although many scholars and practitioners have pledged to work within the traditional three domains of environment, social, and economic conditions, the practical fact is that human life on the planet in almost every political, social, cultural, urban, suburban, or rural context has yet to reach a state of sustainability. In public, government, and professional forums, policy makers and sustainability advocates continue to debate and seek working definitions that will assist in reaching real, sustainable conditions of balance between extractions of the Earth's natural resources and human desires and needs for consumption of those resources. And they continue to debate—sometimes fiercely, resulting in violence and war-like actions—the rights to those resources that are naturally, geographically, or politically limited in availability.

The public's understanding and common use of the term "sustainability" has reached new heights during this quarter of a century. However, divergent uses and wildly differing values and relationships are applied to the language surrounding sustainability, especially when the word "sustain" and its derivatives become verbs intended to describe public actions. The breadth of meanings and interpretations leads to further complexity and often chaotic misunderstandings of an already dynamic, interconnected, interdependent, and holistic framework of management and problem-solving.

Organizational behaviorist Margaret Wheatley provides a snapshot of the dilemma of the 21st century when she says, "The worldview of the sciences ... is no longer hidden in books. It blares from news reports and blazes across our screens in the terrifying images of these times—wars, terrorism, migrations of displaced people, hurricanes, earthquakes, tsunamis. Chaos and global interconnectedness are part of our daily lives. We try hard to respond to these challenges and threats through our governments, organizations and as individuals, but our actions fail us. No matter what we do, stability and lasting solutions elude us. It's time to realize that we will never cope with this new world using our old maps. It is our fundamental way of interpreting the world—our worldview— that must change. Only such a shift can give us the capacity to understand what's going on, and to respond wisely."[5]

The principles of sustainability—especially the more comprehensive view of the five key domains—are composites of a new world view. As such, a new map is needed to find more effective means of navigating the dynamics of change and chaos in the making of cities, communities, and useful products. It is necessary to be able to mark—benchmark —the current status and context and measure the progress toward or

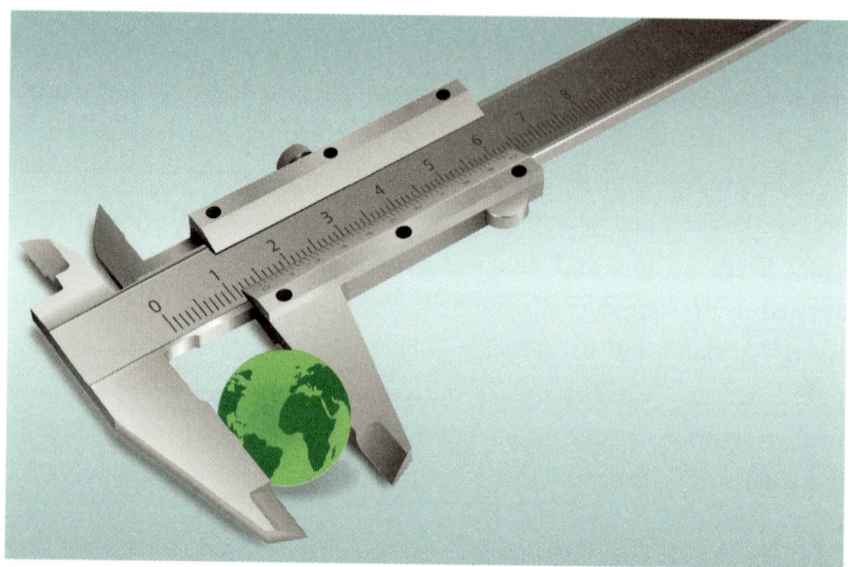

© Diane Wanek / Zigzag Design

away from the goals related to living in sustainable environments on this planet. It has been said that, "We will be able to manage only what we can measure."[6]

The key map that humanity has clung to since early in the 19th century has been the social science of economics. When humans developed the capacity to focus the conversion of energy into the rapid and repetitive making of useful tools and products from the raw resources of the Earth (during the Industrial Revolution), we largely gave standardized practices to the valuation of one resource or one product over another. The common experience of valuing goods and services has led to marketplaces for trade and exchange. Markets and the attempts to maintain their viability have led to the creation of artificial symbols of value for exchange in lieu of the barter of one product for another (money and credit), and the growth and complexity of markets has led to studies and principles of patterns of trade, production, and consumption decisions (economics).

As the patterns of trade, production, and consumption have become more widespread and complex (as seen by virtue of the global economy), a perceived need has developed among nations and centers of commerce to track, evaluate, study, and manage the flow of goods and currencies

© Aldo Murillo / iStockPhoto and Diane Wanek / Zigzag Design

within the economic system. The greater the complexities of interactions and interdependencies have become within this global system. the more elusive the task of managing the economic systems has become. This has given rise to the application by social scientists—economists—of mathematics to the study and forecasting of the economy (econometrics).

As defined by economist Ragnar Frisch in 1933, "Econometrics is concerned with the tasks of developing and applying quantitative or statistical methods to the study and elucidation of economic principles. The field of econometrics has developed methods for identification and estimation of simultaneous equation models. These methods allow researchers to make causal inferences in the absence of controlled experiments."[7]

Economists use econometrics to identify key indicators with related measures of future predicted performances of the various elements of an overall economy. Such indicators and their corollary predictions have become useful in capital, money, and consumption markets to forecast the future flow and demand for goods, services, and resources (i.e., to predict the future value of anything and everything made and marketed by mankind).

What we now are coming to realize through broader visions and better understanding is that the natural resources necessary to continue fueling the industrial making of products for our use and consumption are limited and finite; there are choices to be made if the sustainability of socio-cultures and communities of human inhabitation is our goal.

One choice is to limit the global per capita consumption of natural resources (within a hopeful context of economic business as usual). The means to accomplish this choice would most likely fall into two alternatives: Find the  means to reduce the global and regional populations (although regulatory fiat has not worked in China[8]) or change life style patterns for each

Population density by country

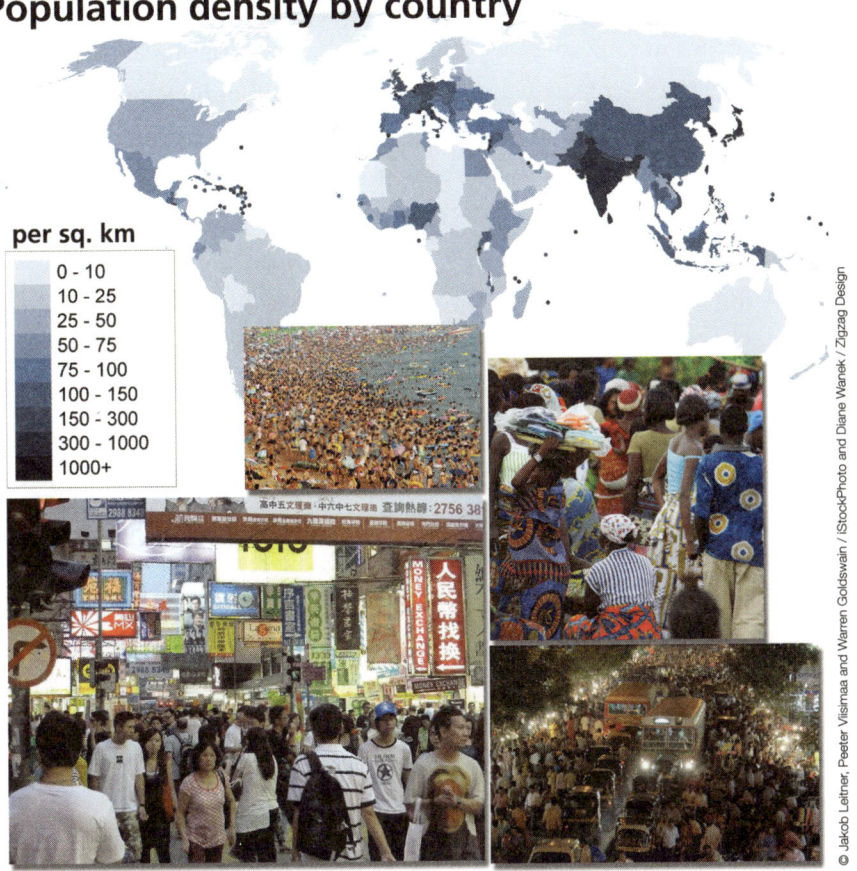

per sq. km

- 0 - 10
- 10 - 25
- 25 - 50
- 50 - 75
- 75 - 100
- 100 - 150
- 150 - 300
- 300 - 1000
- 1000+

person on Earth to diminish his or her rate and volume of consumption of the materials and products produced by others. This choice and both alternatives seem to have particularly draconian implications within the imagined challenges of implementing such reductions.

Economists will predict that such measures would create a global collapse of all markets; social scientists will predict that social chaos would ensue and that regional conflicts would become (even more) violent over competition for limited resources; even environmentalists will acknowledge that such a context would accelerate the destruction of the very resources needing protection; and civic administrators and government officials will be hard-pressed to maintain peace, security, and public order among and between the haves and the have-nots in the relative inequities of such choices.[9] The need and opportunities for new technologies will be diminished, and the global quest for innovation, creativity, and cultural identity will atrophy. In short, the human spirit in most cultures around the world will be thrust into a negative, retrogressive mode.

A third alternative exists: Accelerate the pace and content of education to learn to use a more holistic system of analytics, decision theories, and measurements to the processes of designing, making, using, and reusing goods and products that is based on a conservation ethic rather than a consumption ethic. In short, we need a framework of thinking about the Earth's resources and the appropriation of those resources that will result in reduced consumption of nonrenewable resources while continuing to allow the exercise of the freedoms of innovation and creativity. In this alternative, products and services that contribute to the qualities and equities of human life (within the limits of the resources) for the sustainability of the various cultures of the world would continue to be valued, marketed, and exchanged. Business, industries, productive work, and measureable economies would still exist (even new jobs, opportunities, and markets would be created in a new green economy[10]). Most products and communities would be designed to use renewable resources, and the goal of a sustainable planet would be achieved over time.

The choice and measurement of the indicators of such sustainable intentions and creative decisions would be more comprehensive and outcomes-based than the old world view that fostered the creation of econometrics. The linear, financial-value-above-all-other-values would be expanded and incorporated into a system of balances and interdependences of all the human and eco-system values on Earth. An eco-literacy would be required within all cultures, whether developed, developing, or under-developed. And team-based, comprehensive information about the other four domains will need to be applied to each specific context along with the site-specific eco-literacy. We would call such a system and its related body of knowledge *sustainometrics*.

These new-world metrics—a map for navigating decisions in a context of scarcity and chaos—is based on expansion of the original domains of sustainability and the application of an interactive, simultaneous assessment of the most essential indicators within each domain. Altogether, the process will result in better, conservation-based decisions and the avoidance of many unintended consequences suffered through past trials and errors of judgment about the livable conditions we desire.

CHAPTER 2

It's Not the Economy, Stupid.*
It's Consumption.

In the economics media blitz about the Great Recession that began in 2008, we should be haunted by a headline reading, "Everything that we have learned has turned out to be incorrect." As usual in the popular press, the expression is startling but describing only a partial reality. Almost everyone agrees, however, in the reality of the economic collapse and the dark prospects for a future that will look like the past.

Futurists believe that the darker an issue, the greater the opportunity for innovation.

Such opportunity can be found in our current crisis: A chance for a reformation in our economic beliefs and practices now exists. We have been too single-minded about the economy. Modern economists who believe in a perpetually rising level of consumption and who urge people to buy, consume, throw away, and buy again are preaching a false gospel that the planet cannot support and that will ultimately lead to both economic and environmental bankruptcy.

At the height of the 1983 economic crisis, environmentalist and entrepreneur Paul Hawken wrote in his book *The Next Economy*, "Most people view the growing economic crisis as evidence of something gone wrong. Depending on one's economic philosophy, one can put the blame on various groups and institutions. Conservatives point to the government, monetarists blame the Federal Reserve Bank, Marxists blame the

---

*In the political rhetoric of campaign slogans for the presidential election of Bill Clinton vs. George H.W. Bush in 1992, James Carville coined the phrase, "It's the economy, stupid," for the Clinton campaign, indicating Clinton's intent to emphasize economic recovery as a campaign priority.

capitalist system, politicians blame their predecessors, consumers blame big business and OPEC, and big business has blamed consumers, OPEC and government. Like a losing team, we see only our failures, and as a result, we have turned on one another."[11]

Sound familiar?

In the current crisis, we would place the blame not on the consumer but on the decision processes used by all of us who design, finance, and make consumable products. Consumption has fueled the success of global economies. However, consumption is also the principal contributor to the depletion of natural, nonrenewable resources and most likely to the rate of global warming.

The problem is neither our history and habits of consumption nor that those habits are inherently bad. (We have both needs and desires for consumption of goods and services.) The problem is that our choices frequently harm the environment because of the content, disposal, or consequence to natural materials or systems. The consumer is often not presented with good information as a basis of making good choices, even when we may have adopted a new world view of the future.

The ultimate question for the 21st century is: How can we reduce consumption of nonrenewable materials and sustain the environment in balance with our desired quality of human life?

"The challenge is to redesign the materials economy so that it is compatible with nature," wrote Lester R. Brown, president of the Earth Policy Institute, in his book *Plan B 2.0*. "The throwaway economy that has been evolving over the last half-century is an aberration, now itself headed for the junk heap of history."[12]

Consider your personal behavior as a consumer. Even if you are trying to be green, chances are you will have used and thrown away at least one disposable product today.

According to Giles Slade, author of the book *Made to Break*, Americans invented the concept of disposability with products designed for cheapness, single use, and short-term convenience.[13]

© Braca / Fotolia

© visionsfortomorrow.net

So it's no wonder that the casual throwing away of contact lenses, tissues, razors, batteries, coffee cups, ballpoint pens, diapers, plastic cutlery, paper plates, and even more substantial items such as electronics, microwave ovens, and televisions doesn't even raise an eyebrow.

We've become a throwaway society. Here are some of the numbers:

- 2 million: the number of plastic beverage bottles used in the United States every five minutes.[14]

© ermess / Fotolia

© Aleksey Bakaleev / Fotolia

- 1.14 million: the number of brown paper supermarket bags used in the United States every hour.[15]
- 15 million: the number of sheets of office paper used in the United States every five minutes.[16]
- 1.06 million: the number of aluminum cans used in the United States every five minutes.[17]
- 63 million: the number of working PCs that were trashed in 2003, and that number climbed to 315 million in 2004.[18]

All this adds up to 4.5 pounds of trash per person per day, with each American responsible for trash that approaches one ton each year.[19]

Besides filling up landfills, what other implications do disposables have on the environment? Look at the numbers for disposable coffee cups used in the United States in 2010, courtesy of the Environmental Defense Fund and its Paper Calculator (www.PaperCalculator.org).[20]

- Number of cups used: 23 billion
- Tons of wood consumed: 1.4 million
- Number of trees cut down: 9.4 million
- BTUs of energy used: 7 trillion
- Equivalent number of homes that could be powered: 77,000
- Gallons of water used: 5.7 billion
- Equivalent in Olympic-sized swimming pools: 8,500
- Pounds of solid waste created: 363 million[21]

An alternative is to use manufactured, reusable cups. Even though the initial manufacturing of reusable cups creates a bigger environmental impact than paper cups, the impact lessens over time. After reusable cups have been reused a certain number of times, they become more environmentally friendly than paper cups. One study showed that the environmental impact of a stainless steel mug breaks even with paper cups at 24 uses. Since most reusable mugs are designed for 3,000 uses, the positive environmental impact of reusables can be huge. The creation of waste, the use of natural resources, and damage done by greenhouse gases are all decreased by reusable cups after 24 uses. And reusable cups help cut supply costs for coffee houses, a discount that is often passed on to consumers and saves everyone money, a win-win situation.[22]

People say they buy disposable products for convenience because the products are cheaper, or because they are the only products available for the desired use. In all cases, this is a false economy, as the above example illustrates.

How did American's love affair with disposables begin? In the late 1800s, manufacturers began to realize the commercial potential of short-lived products.[23] Some of the first disposable products, razor blades and condoms, were designed for men, but it was in the marketing to women with products promoted as both hygienic and convenient that a new era in American consumption was born.

During the Depression, marketing campaigns encouraged Americans to replace their automobiles prematurely and buy products to stimulate the economy, culminating in the strange idea of products designed to fail.[24] Enter planned obsolescence, the process of a product becoming obsolete or non-functional in a way that is planned—designed—by the manufacturer.

In the 1950s and '60s, Americans, becoming increasingly affluent, began buying products for novelty rather than necessity.[25]

And following the terrorist attacks of Sept. 11, 2001, President Bush implored Americans to go shopping in an effort to keep the country operating as usual.[26] A similar plea was heard from President Obama during the economic downturn of 2008-'09 in the hope of stimulating the economy back to an approximation of its pre-2008 level.

As Americans buy more and more, hundreds of millions of computers, cell phones, televisions, and other products are disposed of each year. Some of these products are truly obsolete. Some have simply been cast aside in favor of an updated model with new conveniences. Few are designed and manufactured with convenience of repair or longevity in mind.[27]

Advertising historian James Twitchell has said that the problem with

Americans is not that we're materialistic but that we're not materialistic enough.[28] We don't genuinely love our things; what we love is exchanging them for newer things.

Planned obsolescence is helped along when the cost of repairs is similar to the replacement cost or when service or parts are no longer available. But the complete environmental, social, and life-cycle costs are never revealed. Some products may have been designed to have never been serviceable. Creating new lines of products that do not interoperate with older products can also make older models obsolete quickly, forcing replacement.[29]

In other parts of the world, governments and manufacturers are confronting the costs of disposability at long last.

In the United Kingdom, for instance, planned obsolescence engineered into products is considered a breach of customer rights. And there are both public policies and ethical business mores that are designed to protect these rights.[30]

What can be done to combat our cultural programming to spend and dispose?

The new materials economy must be one of reduce, reuse, repair, and recycle, moving the consumption process from the typical three R's to four. We must be smarter, conservation-minded, and more efficient in our decisions. But this intelligence must begin at the conceptual (design) stage of the manufacturing or construction process. The past 25 to 30 years of emphasis on green Earth Day practices and the three R's of conservation have focused on information and education about the end of the energy and materials cycle rather than the beginning.

Three conditions—all elements of the design process—must take more prominence in the making of products and goods for future consumption:

1. Manufacturers, contractors, and goods producers must use more renewable or recycled materials and less nonrenewable materials (especially for big-ticket items such as cars, buildings, appliances, electronics, and mechanical products).

2. All manufacturing processes as well as produced products and their transport to markets must be designed for the maximum possible energy efficiency.

3. All products, goods, and resource uses must be designed for longer life and efficient maintenance, and, if possible, ease of repair or reuse. The waste stream must be reduced to net zero.

If we could accomplish these conditions, the national economy would experience a transformation.

There is a new nonprofit economic development organization, Climate Prosperity Project Inc., which was funded initially by the Rockefeller Brothers Fund, that exemplifies the start of a new green economy transformation. The organization is working to create regional economic development centers in Portland, Ore., St. Louis, Mo., and Washington, D.C.

According to the organization's Web site, "The regional climate prosperity framework includes demand and supply components that together produce multiple economic and environmental benefits:

"The demand component involves building the regional market for clean and green products and services. Activities that create regional demand—from standards to incentives to regulatory policies—are the most common climate prosperity strategies to date.

"The supply component involves growing the regional base of clean and green industries. While a region can increase its market for clean and green products and services, this demand can be met by local firms or firms based outside the region. The more that regional demand is met by local firms, the more economic benefits accrue to the region.

"When a region actively encourages both clean and green demand and supply, it can maximize its environmental and economic benefits: reducing greenhouse gas emissions, improving energy savings, expanding business opportunities, and growing green talent and jobs.

"To complete the framework, an organizational component provides the 'glue' to connect and align both demand and supply strategies and track economic and environmental benefits. A regional 'climate prosperity council' can take many forms—but should reflect the unique characteristics of each region."

The Climate Prosperity Project is an encouraging philosophy and an organized strategy for bringing sustainability principles to the initial economics of manufacturing, trade, and commerce.

What can each one of us—as a single consumer, designer, manufacturer, planner, developer, or community administrator—do to influence and promote this reformation?

The impact on the national patterns of consumption could be huge if every planner, designer, manufacturer, and constructor of components of the built environment used, at the harvesting stage, a sustainability paradigm to guide consumption decisions about nonrenewable and renewable natural resources.

The local and national impact could also be huge if every consumer and voter demanded the display of energy and materials information at the point of purchase, similar to the market's increased content and origin information for processed foods.[31] There are encouraging signs of information-based consumption in some sectors of our existing economy but not nearly enough.

For example, the U.S. Green Building Council's Leadership in Energy and Environmental Design (LEED) building ratings system is a good beginning. It lets consumers know, before construction, what to expect from a building's content and performance.[32] Local, county, state, and national governments could also apply such principles and transparency to governance and the creation and use of public resources if voters demanded the information.

However, product and built environment information for greater consumer awareness will come only from the conceptual—design—stage of the making of goods and services that commerce and industry makes available to the public for consumption. Commerce and industry needs a system of deciding how and when the limited resources will be used to achieve the goal of sustainability; we need a process for decisions that will make conservation-based sense in the making of products, places, communities, and cities. Such a process will be information-dependent, interactive, and interdependent among all the elements of distinguished contexts. It will be measurable over time for the tracking of progress and the responses to the dynamics of change. Such a process might be called *sustainometrics* for shorthand convenience.

The origin and evolution of sustainometrics and the rationale for the information content, based on the five domains of sustainability, recognizes that there is a compelling biological reason to consider the interdependencies of the five domains when we wish to make products and goods from natural resources. The models and application examples presented here will demonstrate that the making of measurements of consumption must occur before the harvesting, manufacture/construction, use, deterioration, and waste cycles begin for human-made products and environments. Sustainometrics performed in this manner will help remind us that all natural material is made up of embodied energy and that there is a natural cycle from growth to use to waste to growth and around again (Figure 11).

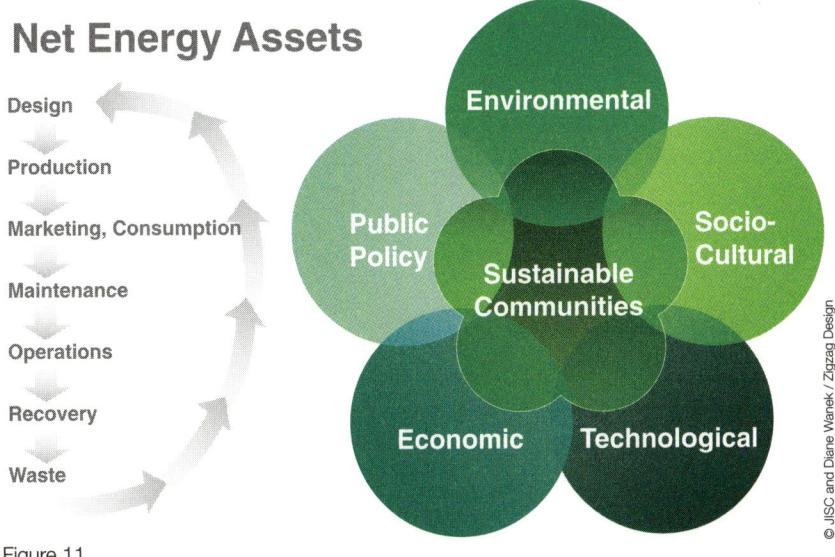

Figure 11

CHAPTER 3

All the World is Local

I n 1992, the first U.N. Conference on Environment and Development (Earth Summit) in Rio de Janeiro produced the Agenda 21 manifesto and other international goals for the protection of the planet.[33]

In 2002, the second Earth Summit produced the U.N. Millennium Development Goals but little new optimism for real global success in achieving the dual goals of the summit, namely, ensuring that economic growth and environmental protection work together, not at odds.[34] It seems that even now, with the third summit upon us in 2012, leaders of the global community of nation-states have not yet developed the political will to lead the people and the globalizing economies into a state of balance. Thus the early optimism for Johannesburg may even turn to regressive behavior from the previous two global summit conferences.

In its "State of the World 2004" report, the U.S.-based Worldwatch Institute reported that the world had begun to respond to the calls of the Rio conference but only "tentatively and unevenly." The authors observed that, "Steps in the 1990s toward a more just and ecologically resilient world were too small, too slow, or too poorly rooted."[35] There are bright spots, even though many national leaders seem not to care about the principles of sustainability. Citizen awareness and concern is growing but mostly at the local level, and many business leaders are discovering that good economics can be sustained and even advanced along with social and environmental improvements. And some units of governments at all levels are reorienting policies and regulations to support the principles of sustainability.

The U.N. Development Program is becoming more influential in expanding people's choices to lead the lives they value, especially choices that foster a long and healthy life, access to education, a decent standard of living, and participation in community life—while strongly advocating for the conservation of resources. And the U.N. Human Settlements Program (UN-Habitat) has become the world's leading resource for Web-based information on global activities and best practices in sustainable development, with more than 1,600 selected examples from around the world of local community development projects that have sustainable characteristics.[36]

In assessing the slow governmental progress toward the goals of the Earth Summits, the numerous broken or unfulfilled treaties between nations—and now the low expectations for future global environmental summits—it appears that the action that will matter most is local action. In any event, numerous cities, neighborhoods, businesses, non-governmental organizations, and individual citizens have assumed the most effective leadership roles for sustainable development in the vacuum of uncoordinated global action by national governments. For instance, the American Institute of Architects found in 2007 that there were more than 90 cities with recently created municipal green building programs throughout the United States.[37]

One example, the Scottsdale, Ariz., Green Building Program stresses the program's function within city government as encouraging "a whole-systems approach through design and building techniques to minimize environmental impact and reduce the energy consumption of buildings while contributing to the health of its occupants."[38] Its principal function is described as the revision and establishment of public policies that "aim to advance green building in the private sector by (1) establishing mandatory green building criteria; (2) providing expedited review as an incentive for green building; or (3) offering other direct financial incentives for green building, including grants, fee waivers, tax breaks, and bonus development."

In addition to the removal of public policy barriers and the creation of new incentive-based policies, the Scottsdale Green Building Program produces public educational and guideline materials in the form of printed handbooks, public presentations, tours, and community television programming. Its educational materials address energy efficiency and retrofitting existing buildings, green guidelines for new construction, green materials and products, green and sustainable landscaping, and more.

Will these local actions be enough, soon enough?

Kofi Annan, Secretary General of the United Nations from 1997 through 2006, painted the worst-case scenario for failure. "Imagine," he said, "a future of relentless storms and floods; islands and heavily inhabited coastal regions inundated by rising sea levels; fertile soils rendered barren by drought and the desert's advance; mass migrations of environmental refugees; and armed conflicts over water and other precious natural resources."[39]

How can the influence of local entities be spread to greater affect? How can we, in any community or world-class city, as political leaders, as business leaders, as educators, professionals, or citizens, mitigate the unintended but disastrous consequence of continuing our consumptive, economics-at-all-costs form of development?

First, **we must believe that individual action matters**, greatly, and that sustainability is a set of principles and values that deserve our utmost, constant, and personal attention. Around the globe, the literature on best practices in both developed and developing societies shows numerous examples of individuals who influence their communities through voice and example with projects of new enterprises, conservation action, green designs, creative governance, and energy efficiencies. We need to lead by committed example with knowledge and awareness, using effective visual, verbal, and electronic communications, and through skill and leadership acumen. We need to accept and understand that leadership for sustainability is not constructed of the same principles or processes as leadership for the economic bottom line.[40]

Second, **we must understand that the world is urbanizing at the most rapid rate in the history of humanity,** and we must attempt to anticipate the consequence of such growth in these urban environments. It is estimated that by 2050, we will see a world of approximately 9 billion people, 70 percent of whom will be living in urban agglomerations.[41] Concurrently, we must seek to understand all the interconnected and interdependent influences and opportunities of an urbanized world.

Third, in this sense of interdependence, **we must appreciate and protect the natural value of the non-urbanized world for the survival of the urbanized world,** especially for agricultural and aquacultural production and the small to mid-size communities that support the production of food and fiber for the nourishment and sustenance of all cultures. Without adequate diet and nutrition—and adequate potable water resources—economic, environmental, or social principles will never attract adequate attention or resources to support a conservation ethic. Small to mid-size communities also provide essential alternatives to urban agglomerations and, as such, offer important cultural qualities to the human habitat.

The Urbanizing World

Equally, or perhaps more important, is the challenge to make the new population centers, the cities of the world and especially the so-called mega-cities, work as sustainable places or at the very least as agglomerations of many sustainable places. Cities have been identified as the major source of air pollution (leading to climate change); of water contamination and depletion of supply (endangering millions of people and causing global conflicts); of excessive fossil fuel consumption (principally because of carbon-based electric power generation and the growth in personal automobiles); of the massive consumption of materials made from nonrenewable resources; and of the depletion of agricultural land through low-density sprawl and expansive waste mis-management. Even the projected depletion of forests and the endangerment of coral reefs can be traced to the excessive consumption of building materials and food preferences in many of the cities of the world.[42]

In July 2009, UN-Habitat Director Anna Tibaijuka outlined a new sustainable urban campaign that is intended to focus the action agendas of the world's cities irrespective of the city's or the nation's profile of development. She declared:

"UN-Habitat has underscored for the past decade ... that sustainable development depends ultimately on sustainable urban development. This message has finally been validated by the findings of the International Panel of Experts on Climate Change. With just half of the world's population living in urban areas, cities already consume over 65 percent of the world's energy, contribute to over 75 percent of all forms of waste, and are directly accountable for over 65 percent of greenhouse gas emissions. The full significance of these findings is yet to be appreciated. ... The 'brown agenda' can no longer be dissociated from the global environmental agenda, popularly known as the 'green agenda.' Cities are, de facto, the frontline actors in meeting the challenges of climate change. Cities have to be part of the solution.

"At the same time, cities hold the single biggest group of people who are vulnerable to the negative effects of climate change. How many of our major cities are coastal or riparian cities? How many of our cities depend on glaciers, forests, and watersheds for water? How many people live in slums, informal settlements, and sub-standard housing whose lives and livelihoods are at risk because of rising sea levels and extreme weather patterns?

"... the World Urban Campaign is devoted to elevating the importance accorded to sustainable urbanisation in global, national, and local policy and decision making. This Campaign is conceived as a partnership endeavor that will harness global knowledge and expertise in support of national and local action. A key component of the Campaign is to revive national Habitat Platforms to stimulate national and local policy dialogue and development for more sustainable and inclusive urban development."[43]

Subsequently, UN-Habitat staff have described the World Urban Campaign as a hearts-and-minds exercise to create a space for the energy, commitment, and ideas of planners and planning organizations to influence policy at local, national, and international levels. In its first year, the Campaign focus will be "Better Cities, Better Lives." The city dimension is crucial because policymakers talk about sustainable development without mentioning its application to cities, yet that is where the majority of the world's population now lives, where most of the carbon emissions are generated, and where there is the best hope of curbing them. In other words: The crisis is urban and the solution is the city.

Today, the need for coordinated, holistic, visionary, and sustainable management of the cities of the world has never been more critical. In the midst of runaway consumption in most of the developed world, inequities and poverty endure in most of the developing world despite ever-growing new science and technologies. The quality of the environment and the quality of life for current and future residents in both the northern and the southern hemispheres are at risk. Balanced and interdependent urban growth management and planning and design for sustainability have become the major challenges of the 21st century for managers, planners, designers, and civic officials.

As communities get larger in both population and land coverage, the expenses of development and maintenance increase disproportionately. The financial support of new growth and its sources becomes more difficult to manage, while new growth at the edges on greenfields drains resources for maintenance and rehabilitation from the older city sections. There are growing economic inequities and social exclusions, internal to the cities, amid dramatic influences from external migrations and informal, illegal settlements, especially in the developing nations.

Conversely, it seems that the greater the economic success of a city or region, the greater the pressures become for social equity in all forms: health, housing, human services, security, employment, income distribution, education, environmental justice. In general, a decent quality of life for all citizens of the urban environment is difficult to achieve. Communities with extreme disparities are not sustainable. Balanced strategies for sustainable urban design and development are essential.[44]

The principles of sustainable urban design, when practiced, help generate cities that are ecologically sustainable (by reducing energy consumption, emphasizing infill, preservation, and reconstruction, eschewing greenfield development), and also socially sustainable (by promoting the individual's social, mental, and physical health and the community's cultural, economic, and social well-being).[45]

Sustainable cities will be creative cities; creative cities will be learning cities. Learning cities will be communities of leaders and participating citizens who learn from all sources of sustainable urban design and development as well as from their experiences and from other sources of best practices. A creative city will be a collective of distinctive, culturally related special places, each with regenerative qualities for the human spirit. The world needs a system of regular communications about the innovations and transferability of new and historic best practices for urban sustainability—for applications in all cultures and nations, both developing and developed.[46]

CHAPTER 4

The Five Domains* of Sustainable Development

I f we are to have a reasonable chance of managing the growth of the urban habitat and at the same time achieve a balance of economic development with the conservation of the Earth's natural systems, we must expand our definition of the principles of sustainability.

We must see the problems in a whole-systems context rather than in a one-dimensional, single-issue context.

During the first official recognition of the concept of sustainable development by the United Nations' Brundtland Commission (formally the World Commission on Environment and Development) in 1987, it was stated that a principle of sustainable development was necessary to protect the natural systems of the Earth and that the principle should "ensure that development meets the needs of the present without compromising the ability of future generations to meet their own needs."[47]

Since the beginning of the concept and the subsequent studies on implementation, sustainable development has consistently been represented as having three domains—the environment, economics, and the social context—and that they must be treated interdependently for a sustainable balance to occur. Many business and governmental leaders have been skeptical about placing any other domain on a par with economics. Even those who sooner or later will adopt the values of living in balance with nature often find the tools and the reach within these three domains to be limited.

---

*In this context, domain is used to mean a field of human activity with similar features, information, or concerns.

The limitations in achieving real sustainability exist whether the scale of the development is at the micro level (such as an individual building or neighborhood) or at the macro scale of habitat (such as a city or a region of urban and community habitats). The designer, planner, developer, civic official, or non-governmental organization leader who is genuinely interested in facilitating a sustainable solution in the urban context will not find all the networks or ingredients, all the information, or all the tools and alternatives for solutions within these three domains only.

Consider, for example, a proposed new development (typically constructed on a greenfield away from the city center) that has all the finance necessary as well as a good environmental plan that protects and restores critical natural ecosystems, and it enhances and improves scores of lives of prospective occupants. However, under new economic and energy limitations on automobile use, it provides no dependable means of affordable transportation to places of employment for residents. The three domains of economics, environment, and social criteria have been treated, but a fourth domain—the technology of transportation—is missing.

In another hypothetical scenario, consider the same development successfully constructed, with adequate public transportation technology and successfully inhabited and operated for some years. Suddenly, a polluting industrial development is authorized for construction on an adjacent site, resulting in health hazards to the residents of the development. In this case, the fifth missing domain is public policy—the regulatory context of the habitat that would have prohibited the conflicting land use and protected public health.[48]

One area of land use policy and administrative policy in the United States that originated from an earlier time and exemplifies unintended negative consequences for sustainable urban development relates to choosing new building sites for public school facilities within urban planning jurisdictions. Many communities across the country have given taxing authority and total administrative control over public school systems—usually grades K-12—to independent boards of education.

This policy of independent separation of funding and managing the local schools from the funding and management of local governments has been protected on the premise that citizen, non-partisan control of the school systems would assure a higher quality of education for the children of the community.

On one hand, we now are witnessing, especially in larger urban contexts, many, many school systems struggling to maintain minimally acceptable educational outcomes and experiences for the K-12 students while also straining to meet the economic and facilities maintenance challenges that good education so greatly needs. Is a policy of independence an appropriate management, leadership, and operational strategy in a time when almost all other human endeavors are seeking synergistic successes from interdependent and cooperative structures?

More explicitly and related to the independent policy of schools in many communities is an operations policy that guides the selection of sites for the location of new school facilities. It has become standard practice for school system planners to attempt to anticipate future growth directions of the city and to be the first to acquire developable property in key locations in advance of other development or land use interests. Their criteria for selection and purchase are not dissimilar from the private developer's interests. The school system wants the best location at the cheapest price (to protect the public's economic interests, they claim); they want good topographic features, such as adequate drainage, buildable terrain, stable soil, and flexible orientation of buildings and playground sites on the campus; they want good vehicular access and assurance from the city for inexpensive access to city utilities and publically maintained infrastructure.

In the exercise of such policies, the independent school system becomes the advance scout for urban sprawl due to the dual motivations to acquire land at the least cost and to work with local developers to assure that the necessary rooftops with young children beneath will ultimately surround the school site for both population and property tax dollar incomes to support the new school. This greenfield approach for new schools at the edge of the community drains resources and vitality from the heart of cities and accelerates the environmental deterioration and the flight from the older, more dense land uses in urban neighborhoods.[49]

Within the two domains of technology and policy, there are numerous other examples of human invention or intervention that have either facilitated or blocked community progress toward sustainability. Two extreme, and admittedly debatable, examples are the technology of the automobile (and the consequences of its use resulting in threats to the natural systems) and the policy of land ownership (and the consequential effect of economic speculation on the Earth's natural systems). Whether or not we individually value these conditions is not the key consideration in this particular discussion. A fact of modern life is that technologies exist, that they are influential and have been historically important, and that they will continue to accelerate through human ingenuity. So too will the rules and regulations for relations among us and our access to the bounties of the Earth. Both domains are pervasive and affective. The cause-and-effect relationships to the other three domains are inseparable from them.

A further limitation in the classic three-domain definition of sustainability is the often limiting or limited view of the social domain. In the context of globalized economics, it is often the case that cultures, cultural histories, or public aspirations for maintenance of cultural distinctions are either accidentally or intentionally overlooked.

From the beginning of the 20th century and continuing today at an accelerated pace, global cultures have become more homogenous and less distinct than in any previous era of history. Architectural expressions have become more similar and Westernized and less respectful of distinct, historical cultures. Telecommunications and computer technologies have provided instantaneous exchanges of information among cultures, and the multitude of technologies fueling the engines of global economics have provided almost instantaneous access to goods and materials regardless of their place of origin or manufacture. Cultural images and symbols can now be instantly mixed, matched, modified, and reformatted into virtual images that may or may not convey valuable or lasting cultural information. But the images nevertheless are highly influential. Not only have these systems of instant availability overwhelmed many indigenous cultural patterns but they are also, in unintended consequential ways, overwhelming the natural systems of the Earth.[50]

The social domain must always provide for a reminder—and the tools for analysis—of not only the quality of life of people but also their cultural heritages, aspirations, and symbols. Decision leaders need to be reminded of the essential nature of distinctive cultures, and they need effective tools to read and describe the variety of cultures that constitute the human habitat—thus, the proposed modified socio-cultural domain.

On the basis of these and other examples of mankind's continuing and widening gulf of separation between human systems and natural systems, the Joslyn Institute has developed project evidence through models and case studies in repetitive scales of development that the five domains of sustainability form the essential foundation for all deliberations of sustainometrics, and they are, as earlier defined (and illustrated in Figure 12)[51]:

- Environmental (natural and man-made)

- Socio-cultural (history, conditions, and contexts)

- Technological (appropriate, sustainable)

- Economic (the production of goods and services within a sustainable context and the financial resources to support the production, trade, operations, and maintenance)

- Public policy (government, or public rules/regulations)

Figure 12. The five domains of sustainability

Five Domain Characteristics of Sustainable Cities and Communities

Truly sustainable cities will be creative cities made up of many distinct characteristics within the five domains of sustainability.[52]

Within the **environmental domain,** it will be essential to ensure that the habitat has adequate and clean air, water, and sanitation. There will be an abundance of environmentally protected, accessible green spaces and recreational areas as well as products, goods, and services that are free of pollutants and greenhouse gases and protective of the local nonrenewable natural resources. Adequate habitats for the natural flora and fauna of the region must be protected.

Within the **socio-cultural domain** there must be an atmosphere of respect for cultural, spiritual, and ethnic diversity, safe and affordable housing, health care for all citizens, and exceptional educational programs and facilities to accommodate lifelong creative endeavors. The indicators of socio-cultural sustainability must provide for maximum opportunities for human growth and development irrespective of existing economic conditions.

Within the **technological domain** there must be applications and availability of appropriate and affordable technologies: carbon-free and efficient energy systems, convenient and efficient mass transit, functioning and sustainable buildings and infrastructures, and ubiquitous communications systems. The technologies applied must not diminish—or contribute to a net loss of—natural resources.

Within the **economic domain** there must be a dynamic atmosphere of locally owned enterprises with both local and export market goals that support meaningful and fairly compensated employment. There must be a balanced and definitive connection to the other four domains.

And in the **public policy domain** the rules and regulations for developing, operating, and sustaining a creative city must be designed and administered in open, transparent, and participatory ways to support the balance and coordinated effectiveness of all five of the domains.

Further, in the city of the future these domains should be the organizing principles for urban administration, urban design and planning, urban growth management, and regional and urban sustainable development. The domains and all the information contained within them are interdependent, interactive, and affective, one in turn upon each of the other four. A systematic analysis of their interdependencies and the measurement of their several indicators of progress toward sustainability in any developmental or operational situation will reduce the potential of unintended, unanticipated consequences at any scale of development.

Are Resilient Communities Also Sustainable Communities?

In some locations around the globe, there are scholars and practitioners who are promoting a language of resilience to describe desirable community characteristics in the face of the apparent coming of climate changes. In such practices, it often seems convenient to substitute "resilient" for "sustainable." This substitution of language appears to us to be potentially misleading and detrimental to an ultimate goal of achieving comprehensive sustainable conditions for any particular community, especially if the five domains principles are acknowledged as the intellectual and information foundations of a sustainable community.

Sustainability in the original U.N. Brundtland Commission's language was never intended to be defined only as a system that can keep going under normal circumstance. The call for global action was about the abnormal condition of humankind using and fouling the planet's resources in such a manner that threatens the well-being of future generations.

The definition of "resilience" implies reaction—reaction to external forces or conditions to return to normalcy. Certainly, there is a place for conditions of resiliency in the qualities of communities, especially in circumstances of preparations for or recovery from natural disasters or in conditions of political upheaval. However, the appeal for sustainable development is about proactive human behavior with an intent to repair and prevent future damage of the kind we have already inflicted upon the Earth's natural systems. To be merely resilient lets us off the hook of shared responsibility for these damages.

The recent paper "Community Vitality: The Role of Community-Level Resilience, Adaptation, and Innovation in Sustainable Development," published in January 2010 (Dale, Ling and Newman)[53], reports on a study of 35 Canadian communities and their progress toward becoming sustainable communities. The authors comment, "In our research tracking positive community level efforts to encourage sustainable development in a wide variety of fields such as transport, energy, and infrastructure, we found examples that strongly suggest that it is at the community scale that the application of innovation, both techno-logical and social occurs most effectively, and, when aggregated has the greatest impact in increasing sustainability at a broader scale."

Their study also reports, "Some communities … remain strong in the face of external challenge. They possess what we call community vital-ity; they are resilient, they are innovative, and they are adaptive. Simply put, a vital community is one that can thrive in the face of change. It is a place that can remain at its core a functional community without loss to ecological, social, and economic capitals in the long run, whatever occurs as a result of exogenous changes beyond its control. And perhaps more importantly, it is a place where human systems work with rather than against natural systems and processes."

Although resilience, innovation, and adaptability are acknowledged in this study as characteristics of certain communities, these terms are not standalone conditions and should not be described apart from the goals and conditions of sustainable development if we wish to sustain our natural systems and communities in balance as quality places.

Degrees of resilience can be accomplished and measured without nec-essarily having achieved overall sustainability of the whole community. However, a condition of measured, comprehensive sustainability can-not be achieved unless the community and its components also achieve measured resilience to the external conditions (i.e., global warming). If we are listing component goals, strategies, or elements of community sustainability, then we would agree that resilience should appear but not as an equal or alternative to sustainability.

How then will we know when a component of the built environment, especially human habitats such as cities or neighborhoods that take years to develop and construct, are either more or less sustainable? How can we measure the component characteristics of resilience, innovation, and adaptability to gain a comprehensive view of the community's sustain-ability? We need a system of performance metrics—sustainometrics, if you will—to assess the present, chart the future, and track the course.

Applying Sustainability Indicators and the EcoSTEP℠ Tool

To define and create a system of sustainometrics, we first need to develop the proper tools. Measuring or projecting the improvement or decline of various quality-of-life and quality-of-environment factors over time is clarified using the EcoSTEP℠ tool, first developed at the Joslyn Institute in 2004 in response to the challenges of analyzing the growth management issues within the local Flatwater Metroplex. Symbolizing the cyclical quality and interconnectivity of all living systems, EcoSTEP℠ is an effective tool for plotting various sustainability indicators in three term, or time, ranges—short, mid, and long—each divided into 10 time frames that can be defined by user-chosen criteria (i.e. one year, 10 years, etc.).[54] (Figure 13)

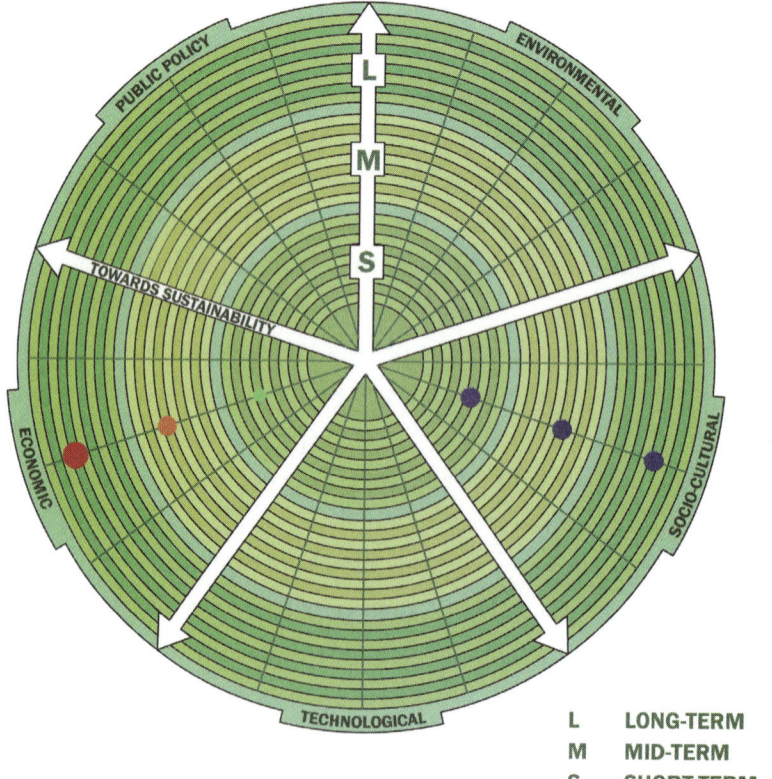

L	LONG-TERM
M	MID-TERM
S	SHORT-TERM

Figure 13. The EcoSTEP℠ tool for measuring sustainability

In an ideal world, an indicator (for example, water quality), plotted near the outermost ring of each term scale would be judged to be approaching the best possible outcome or condition for sustainability.

In this example, short-term conditions appear to be approaching optimal, yet the relative immediacy of mid- and long-term measures indicate water quality challenges that lie ahead. For further detail, the dots plotted on the scale can be color-coded and sized according to the urgency or scale of the challenge of that particular indicator.

The EcoSTEP^{SM} tool allows any user to assess hypothetical or real-life situations, or real conditions of design or planning intent, to assess the assumptions for consequences and trade-offs, and to communicate those situations to stakeholders and leadership. By incorporating all five domains, the tool is effective both in gauging progress and revealing the various and complex trade-offs that will occur between indicators.

This graphic representation of issues and conditions makes EcoSTEP^{SM} an ideal tool for collaborative planning as well as for communicating to leaders and the public a region's (or a building, district, neighborhood, or city's) progress toward a sustainable vision and quality-of-life goals.

CHAPTER 5

Examples of Places and Systems, the Variety of Uses of the EcoSTEP^SM Tool

T he Joslyn Institute has applied the EcoSTEP^SM tool to a diverse range and scale of built-environment projects, including individual buildings, neighborhoods, small communities, districts within cities, and large regions. The tool has been effectively used in pre-design programming, neighborhood and regional assessments, post-occupancy evaluations of individual buildings, and comparative analyses of similar buildings.

A particularly extensive application of the tool occurred in September 2006 during a charrette that brought together 150 architects, planners, and regional stakeholders to identify growth challenges and opportunities and to envision a sustainable future for a rapidly growing metroplex region. The charrette participants were divided into six groups, simultaneously examining six environments in an urbanizing region in southeast Nebraska dubbed the Flatwater Metroplex. The six environments included:

- I-80 interstate highway corridor environs: Examination of growth challenges and opportunities at various sites along the Interstate 80 corridor between Lincoln and Omaha/Council Bluffs

- Communities in the path of growth: The impacts/opportunities of growth in a small commuter town between Lincoln and Omaha

- Suburban conservation community: Proposal for a conservation community near Bennington (exurban Omaha)

- Transformation of a regional shopping mall: Outdated suburban retail area in a mid-sized metroplex community

- Urban core center: An examination of opportunities for revitalization in downtown Lincoln associated with the Downtown Master Plan, Antelope Valley Project, and other work and studies

- Near urban core neighborhood: Continuing the revitalization of the Drake Court district near downtown Omaha based on other recent Joslyn Institute studies and improvements in this historic neighborhood (Figures 14-19)

The charrette teams, with the help of trained facilitators, each identified a minimum of 15 sustainability indicators (three each for the five domains) for the six projects. This work formed the basis of new design/planning programs for the six projects and established the foundation of measurable sustainability actions for future development of the six proposals.

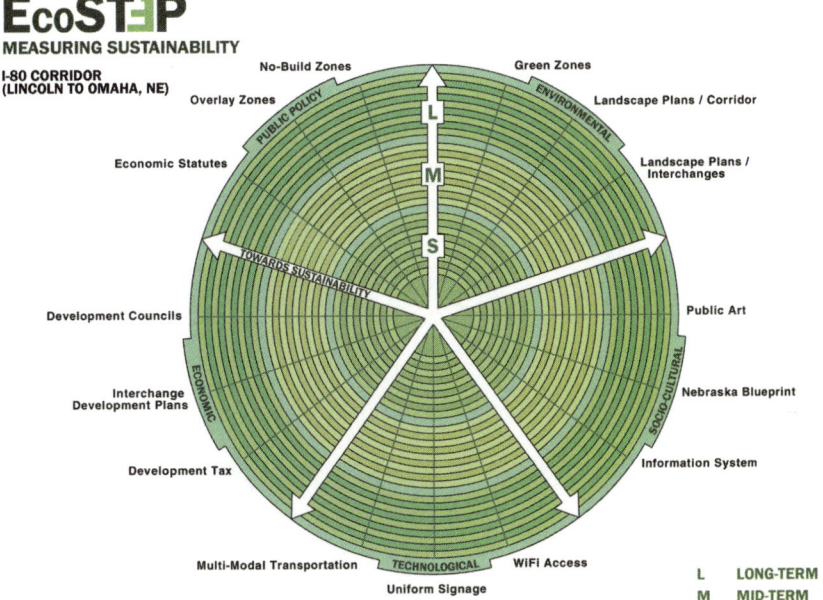

Figure 14. Regional interstate highway corridor

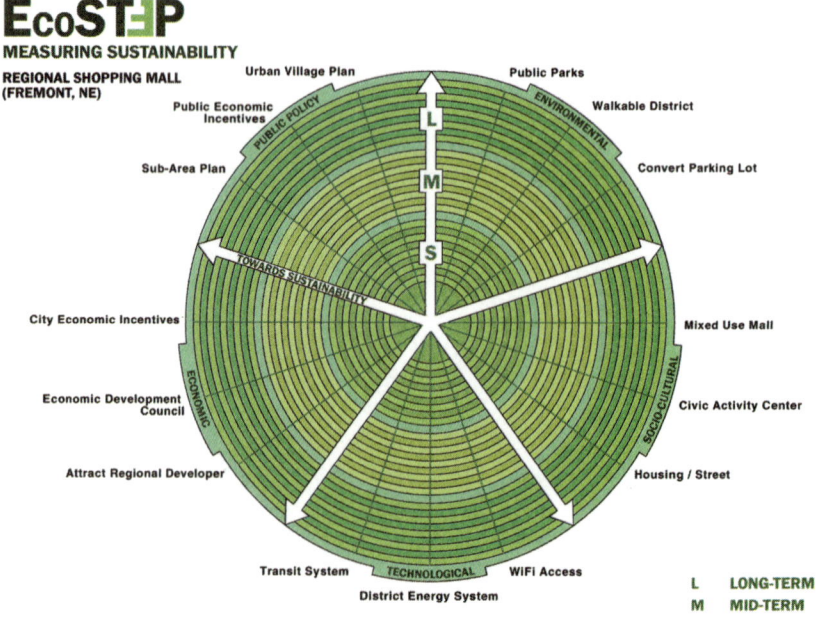

Figure 15. Retrofit of big box shopping center

© Robert Hanna

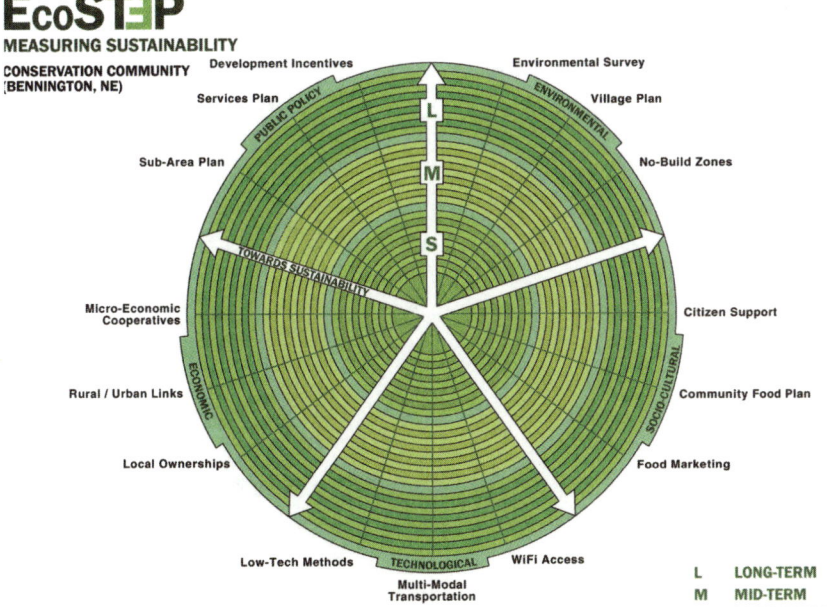

Figure 16. Mixed-use suburban development

Figure 17. Revitalization of midtown urban core

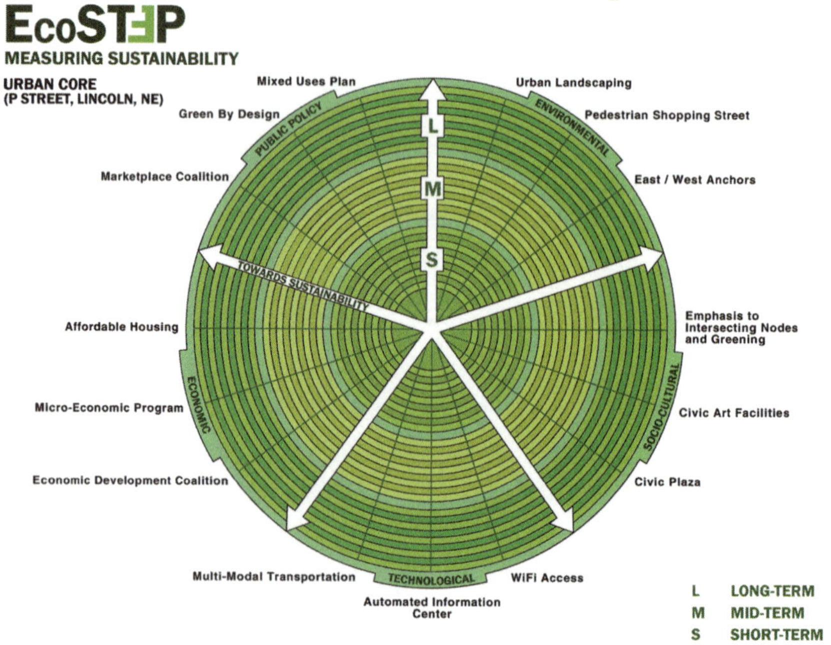

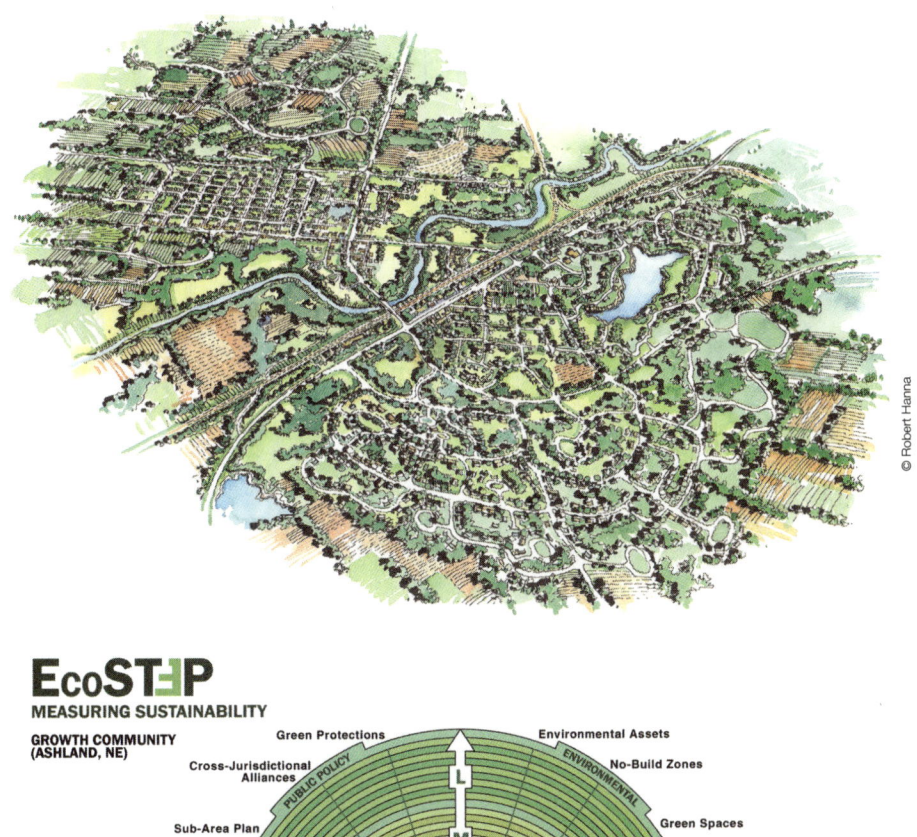

Figure 18. A small community in the path of growth

© Robert Hanna

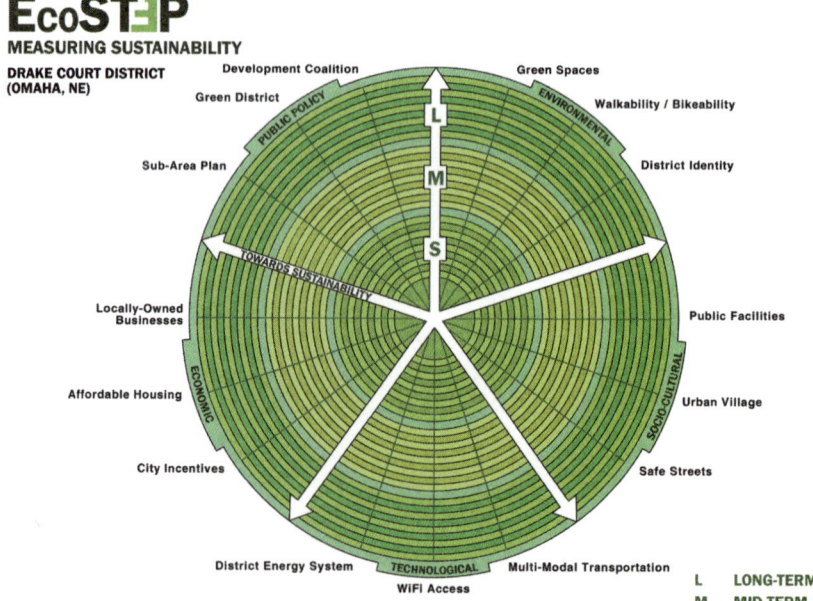

EcoSTEP

MEASURING SUSTAINABILITY

DRAKE COURT DISTRICT
(OMAHA, NE)

Development Coalition

Green District

PUBLIC POLICY

Sub-Area Plan

Green Spaces

ENVIRONMENTAL

Walkability / Bikeability

District Identity

TOWARDS SUSTAINABILITY

L

M

S

Locally-Owned
Businesses

ECONOMIC

Affordable Housing

City Incentives

SOCIO-CULTURAL

Public Facilities

Urban Village

Safe Streets

District Energy System

TECHNOLOGICAL

WiFi Access

Multi-Modal Transportation

L   **LONG-TERM**
M   **MID-TERM**
S   **SHORT-TERM**

© JISC / ArchRival

Figure 19. Revitalization of an urban district

In any practical application of these models to actual planning of similar projects, the next step in the use of the EcoSTEP℠ tool would be to plot the existing sustainability indicators on the EcoSTEP℠ graph. This action would set up the decision-making process for the mid- and long-term scales of future progress toward sustainability.

These six distinct environments are models for the many types of rural and urban communities that require evaluations and design/planning for new conditions of sustainability. Challenges and solutions identified through the use of the EcoSTEP℠ tool are readily transferable to any community facing growth and change.

Applying Sustainability Indicators: The Key to Sustainometrics

One of the six envisioning regional design charrettes, the revitalization of an urban commercial district (i.e., the Drake Court District in Omaha, Neb.), has been selected as a case study to illustrate the use and conditions of the sustainability indicators.[56] The 15 indicators (three for each of the five domains) were selected by the charrette facilitator and the Josylyn Institute staff following the charrette team's completion of design and planning recommendations. As noted above, each team, with the assistance of a professional facilitator, worked through the five domains to identify strengths, weaknesses, opportunities, and threats to the existing urban district. The discussions and the body of text, drawings, and illustrations produced by the charrette team served as the foundation for selection of the indicators.

Drake Court Sustainability Indicators

Environment
- Increase green and public open spaces; increase green streetscapes
- Enhance conditions for walkability, bikeability, and overall connectivity to adjacent districts and pedestrian destinations
- Upgrade the building stock; give the district a distinct visual and socio-cultural identity.

Socio-Cultural
- Develop new mixed uses; create a character of an urban village; emphasize mixed-income housing with commercial facilities to accommodate daily needs.
- Create safe streets and public gathering places; create a new downtown civic plaza for Omaha.
- Emphasize and accommodate public facilities; extend the arts corridor along 20th Street.

Technological
- Begin planning for a new multi-modal transit and transportation system for the district and downtown.
- Make Wi-Fi electronic access available throughout the district.
- Develop feasibility plans for a district energy and utilities system.

Economic
- Create city government incentives for the development of infill and new development for the district.
- Emphasize the economics of affordable and low-income housing connected to development incentives for daily needs shops and stores.
- Give priority to developments with locally owned businesses.

Public Policy
- Incorporate a new sub-area plan for the district into the city's comprehensive plan.
- Develop an overlay plan for the district designating the district "green by design."
- Create a district citizen's development coalition with members from property owners, stakeholders, businesses, institutions, and residents in the district.

The measurable sustainability indicators can be identified and validated in a variety of ways. In design or planning project contexts, the most likely method would be through a facilitated consensus of gathered stakeholders (as in the Drake Court example). In a broader, community-wide context, the sustainometrics director might employ an initial step of statistically surveying the community for majority opinions of the key indicators. In a context of product design and manufacturing, the sustainometrics director might engage a focus group of potential users, designers, and stakeholders of the product in question to identify the most essential indicators in each domain.

Selecting relevant and measurable indicators from each of the five domains is the key to the metrics of sustainability in the system of sustainometrics. There are two required and essential characteristics for each indicator:

- Each indicator should have a data set and a topology of measurable information by which the condition, event, or circumstance can be described and evaluated.

- The source of the data should be available over time for tracking and comparative purposes. The information should be available periodically in a consistent format.

The EcoSTEP℠ graphic illustrations (Figures 20 and 21) show the 15 indicators and the assessment of short-term (or existing), mid-term, and long-term prospects of contributing to a more sustainable condition for each. Figure 21 shows an example of pulling one domain away from the other four for a special focus of the interaction of the sustainability indicators within one domain. However, the separation exercise in this example does not imply any validation to the return of single-issue strategies for planning and design.

Six of the indicators have been given values of highest priority for required action (identified by the size and color of the plot points). If these actions are not accomplished or if other indicators are assigned higher values, then the related indicator values will change and the time/action plot points will indicate a variety of consequences, most likely as threats to the overall sustainability of the project. Assuming that the six priority indicators will receive the resources and the attention required, other related indicators will benefit and gain new values as well as new priorities for the overall related success of the project and its sustainable future. New plots on the diagram and the sustainability indicator lines, say on an annual basis, will provide good communications to all stakeholders about progress throughout the life of the project.

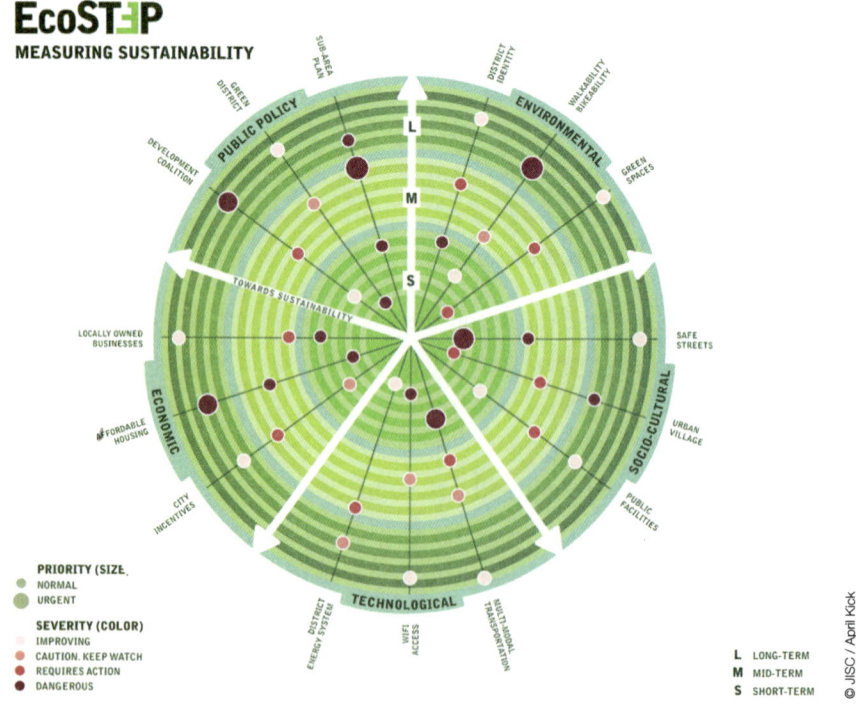

Figure 20. Metrics of sustainability indicators for Drake Court, Omaha, Neb.

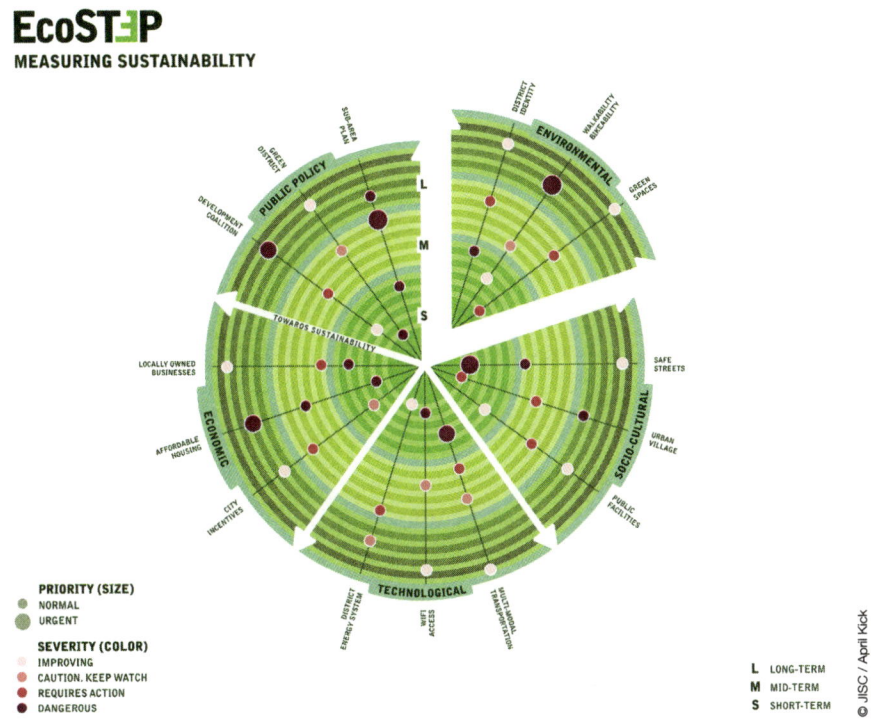

Figure 21. Three indicators, each domain; focus on single domains in the process of analysis of interdependent conditions

Indicators of What and by Whom?

An essential content characteristic of sustainability indicators in the scheme of sustainometrics is that each indicator must be a marker—a measurable component—of the condition of being or becoming sustainable. This means that each must be sustainable from an environmental conservation perspective, sustainable from a socio-cultural human quality-of-life perspective, sustainable from the perspective of uses of appropriate and renewable technologies, sustainable in economic monetary and value-added measures, and sustainable in the sense of good government, equitable policies, and a regulatory environment that promotes freedoms that lead to innovations and creativity.

The most sustainable condition will result when these indicators are recognized for their interdependence and are in relative balance with each other over defined dimensions of time.

"Sustainability indicators" has taken on multiple meanings in a similar fashion to the many definitions now purported for "sustainability." There are practitioners who attempt to make a science of defining indicators; there are organizations that are dedicated to cataloguing and standardizing language and characteristics of indicators; and there are those who use the language of sustainability indicators to argue for the preferred prominence of one domain over another (i.e., environmentalism over economics or economics over social conditions).

A relatively new organization, Global Cities Indicators Facility (GCIF) at Toronto University, Canada, is having considerable success creating a network of global cities for purposes of choosing and comparing city-to-city uses of various pre-determined indicators. The project is functioning under the sponsorship of the World Bank. Its mission is broadly stated: "The Global Cities Indicators Program is designed to help cities monitor performance and quality of life by providing a framework to facilitate consistent and comparative collection of city indicators. The program includes a set of indicators that are standardized, consistent, and comparable over time and across cities."

The GCIF data collection and reporting system is established to cover two categories: city services and quality of life. Multiple themes of data points have been established under each of the two categories, with guidelines for the collection and reporting of the data within each of the pre-determined themes. While this framework seems to be providing member cities with a good, standardized system of collecting and reporting vital statistics, the results of the data system do not seem to reveal inherently and interdependently the comprehensive sustainability profile of any one single community.

As has been previously stated, data collection, storage, and updating are absolutely essential to maintaining a system of sustainometrics.

Every community will benefit from efficient and relevant data systems. However, our view of the process of identifying the most relevant indicators for sustainability is that it functions best when identification comes from local inhabitants, not "experts" in a pre-determined format in isolation from the local conditions and heritage. The intense and interactive process required for neighborhood-by-neighborhood, district-by-district, community-by-community, or city-by-city identification of the most relevant and interdependent indicators will lead to a social, community development-based discourse. Such discourse and human engagement in identifying and working toward the most desirable qualities of a community is a necessary hallmark of a sustainable community. The most creative cities will be distinctive places with distinctive measures of their places and their progress toward sustainable conditions.

Creative City Outcomes

Cities are not built in a day, nor are they constructed of whole cloth. Urban development is dynamic, incremental, and evolutionary. The creative city will be an amalgam of connected, interdependent—but distinctive, high-quality—and culturally diverse places. More often than not, traditional developer-driven or growth-at-all-costs planning, design, and administration loses sight of long-term sustainability and the essential interdependencies and connections that are so necessary to creative cities. The EcoSTEP^SM tool is a means to simultaneous deliberation of these complexities and to long-term, coordinated urban development.[57]

Within this recommended methodology for designers, planners, and urban administrators it is imperative that the user adopt the five domains principles of sustainability. This cognitive framework will prompt the user to consider a more thorough brief on the limitations, information, and interdependent opportunities for the goal of creating sustainable products, places, and habitats.

Viewed aggregately and measured annually (or on any regular time cycle), the EcoSTEP^SM tool can be used:

- In design/planning for the project context by professionals

- As an organizing mechanism for an interdisciplinary team

- As an information vehicle between city administration and project stakeholders

- As a public information vehicle for annual or cyclical progress reports

- As a post-occupancy evaluation instrument for specific projects and developments as they are completed in the community context

We can see how this tool can be applied to an emerging urban area in the American heartland, but how does it hold up when applied to the massive urban agglomerations that are becoming the norm all over the globe and particularly in the developing world? As we shall see, the tool proves remarkably flexible at virtually any scale and can reveal the potential for sustainability in even the most complex and rapidly changing urban environments.

From 2008 through 2010, the Joslyn Institute conducted 22 workshops for elected officials and community leaders across Nebraska to broaden the understanding and the potential uses of the EcoSTEP[SM] tool in community development and public administration.[58] The response to the modeling exercises on alternative uses conducted during these workshops has been wide-ranging and enthusiastic. But, you may say, these are small places compared to urban agglomerations and mega-cities. Are there applications for the urban contexts?

In 2002, we were invited to send a representative to the Shanghai Mayor's Business Advisory Council.[59] Preparation for our presentation on sustainable development provided us the opportunity to analyze the question of applications in a mega-city.

Figure 22. City Center, Shanghai

Shanghai and Other Mega-Cities: Is Sustainability Possible?

In the context of urban history, Shanghai has been one of the most sustainable habitats on Earth, growing from village status in 700 A.D. to the world-class and mega-city size of almost 17 million residents today.[60] The engines of environmental location and resources, economics, culture, and advancing technologies have largely driven the growth of Shanghai and other major cities of today—especially through the 18th, 19th, and 20th centuries. However, in a world of growing demands and limited resources, will there be enough food, potable water, fossil fuel energy, and natural and economic capital for the sustained support of the projected population and all their desires and enterprises? How can we strike a balance between a growing population with escalating desires for consumption and the current rate of depletion of the Earth's resources?

These questions are relevant to every community on the globe—north, south, developed, or developing, small, large, mega, or intermediate in size. We are leaving the era when the international argument has been over poverty or rich versus poor. This language is from the Industrial Revolution, economics-above-all-else thinking, which symbolizes only one measure among the five domains. The rich may have significant economic wealth but may be poor in environmental resources or sociocultural attributes; the poor may have less economic stature but may be wealthy in cultural history and basic quality of life. (This scenario, however, is not intended to deny the fact that there are extremes in the imbalances, nor that history has recorded numerous cultures and communities that could not sustain themselves due to the extreme imbalances.)

The desired balance can only come from a system of values that seeks to balance and represent each of the five domains in all endeavors regardless of whether the values are expressed through problem identification and assessment, problem solving, design, planning, management, or administrative frameworks. Bundling the five domains in both language and principles of organization will guide these endeavors into a consistent and constant awareness of whole-systems strategies. In the past, institutions, organizational structures, science, and technology have been approached largely through compartmentalized, incremental, often independent, and task-centered descriptions. Frequently, such regimes of management have led to unintended, unanticipated consequences, inefficiencies, bureaucratic duplication, or social collapse and very often to irreparable damages to the surrounding natural systems.

Shanghai, not unlike most cities of the world, has organized its government around the separated increments of tasks, such as education, health, justice, taxation, housing, tourism, and agriculture. (Its municipal Web site lists more than 60 such offices and agencies as units of the Municipality of Shanghai.) Without more personal experience with this city government or a more creditable basis for research and understanding, it is impossible for us to know the assets and liabilities of this particular structure. We do know from considerable personal experience over the past 30 years with the Chinese culture and other research and practice experiences with smaller U.S. and international cities organized in similar ways, that coordination of any of the task-defined agencies is extremely difficult. The success in coordinated actions for sustainable development very much depends on the skill, style, and values of individual leaders in governmental offices. More often than not, the outcomes of planning and administration that have any similarity to truly sustainable, balanced conditions will be more accidental and less permanent than pre-planned and long-term. Continuity in coordination and sustainable conditions under these circumstances of political and leadership dynamics is extremely difficult to achieve.

Sustainable Urban Governance[61]

Envision, for the sake of discussion, that city government could be organized not around the idea of the performance of critical tasks but around the outcomes expectation of balanced sustainability. This expectation would be pervasive, shared by all leaders, managers, civic officials, and most important of all, by the public and principal stakeholders of the city. Coordination and team engagement would replace independence, specialization, duplication, and competition. Long-range planning would replace expedience, trial and error, crisis management, and indecisiveness. Imagine a sustainable development governance model that defined a council of administrators of each of the five domains of sustainability—environment, socio-cultural, technological, economic, public policy—plus, a division of administrative services to supply the professional and special human talents required to implement and maintain the development patterns.

Leaders of this sustainable development council would be specifically selected for having the requisite knowledge, values commitment, and political will to support eco-systems design and management. In return, they would be supplied with the human and fiscal resources and the support of the local stakeholders to implement and sustain the necessary eco-system policies for the city or community. These attributes and resources will be required to implement and coordinate new visions for future development, maintenance of existing valued infrastructure, and growth management for a sustainable city, or on a micro-scale, for a collection of sustainable neighborhoods and places. Perhaps most significant of all, such a system of urban management would give future generations a workable framework for development rather than a wasted inheritance.

Obviously, the already identified municipal tasks must be accomplished. Education, for instance, is essential. But within a sustainability paradigm should not education be framed through the coordinated, interdependent framework of the five domains? If the outcome of the city efforts in education were expected to be lifelong in duration, inclusive for all citizens, and guided by the aim of public participation in the goals of a sustainable society (or some other broad, coordinated goals established by a sustainable development council), then we suspect that not only would the education experiences and administration be different but so too would the city. It is conceivable that every task-oriented agency or department currently defined for a city's administration could be realigned to one of the six units (the five domains plus administrative services) of a sustainable development council (Figures 23-28).

Agency Examples

- water conservation bureau
- agriculture commission
- environmental protection
- assets management
- grain bureau
- agriculture and forestry
- landscaping
- housing & land resources
  management

Figure 23. Environmental domain agency examples

Agency Examples

- education commission
- ethnic and religious
  affairs
- civil affairs
- labor/social security
- culture, radio, film, t.v.
- health bureau
- family planning
- sports

Figure 24. Socio-cultural domain agency examples

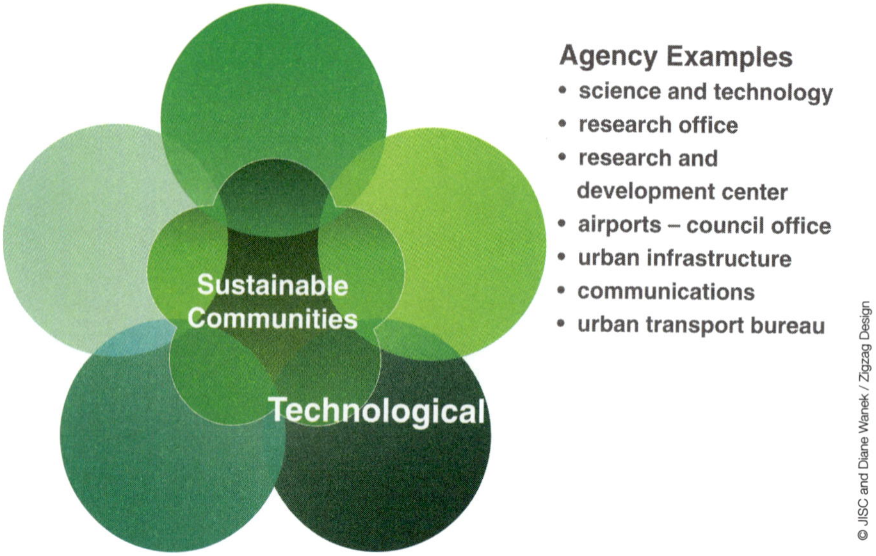

Sustainable Communities
Technological
Agency Examples
• science and technology
• research office
• research and development center
• airports – council office
• urban infrastructure
• communications
• urban transport bureau
© JISC and Diane Wanek / Zigzag Design

Figure 25. Technological domain agency examples

Agency Examples
• price bureau
• economic commission
• commercial commission
• finance bureau
• taxation bureau
• foreign trade
• foreign investment
• tourism
• international shipping
Sustainable Communities
Economic
© JISC and Diane Wanek / Zigzag Design

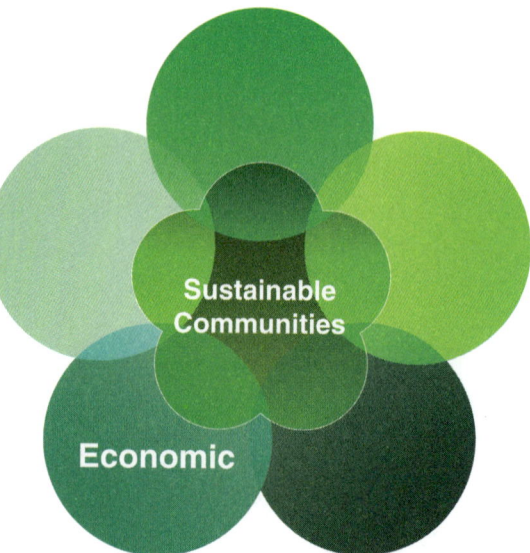

Figure 26. Economic domain agency examples

Agency Examples

- liason office
- justice bureau
- coordinating office
- overseas Chinese affairs
- legislative affairs
- counselors' office

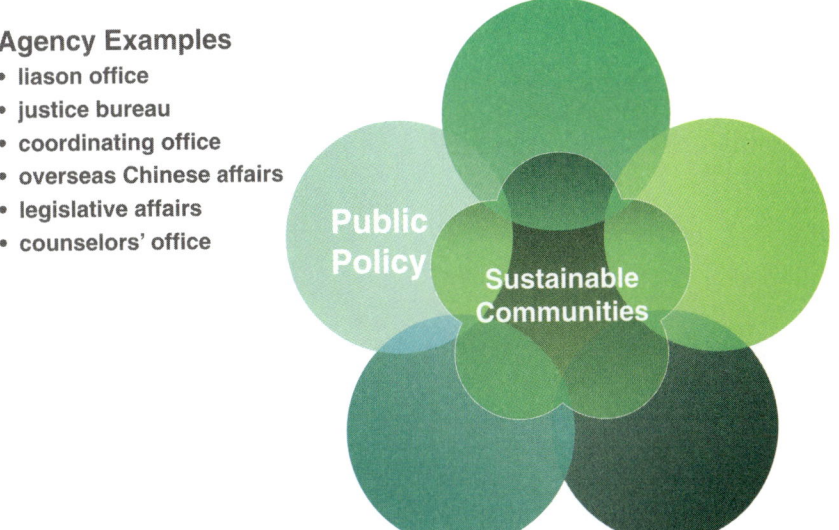

© JISC and Diane Wanek / Zigzag Design

Figure 27. Public policy domain agency examples

Agency Examples

- development planning
- public security
- state security
- commission of supervision
- personnel bureau
- construction & management
- audit bureau
- statistics
- urban planning
- press & publication
- copyright administration
- intellectual property

© JISC and Diane Wanek / Zigzag Design

Figure 28. Administrative services agency examples

CHAPTER 6

Learning and Practice Tips: Sustainability Indicators

Whether the goal is good public health within a context of sustainable development or sustainable development planned around an environment of a healthy city, it seems the two are inseparable, and practically speaking, they are interchangeable for governance purposes. In any event, whether we are planning for regional cities, healthy cities, or sustainable cities, there are new planning paradigms that emerge:

- **Coordination and cooperation.** Single-sector and individual, independent task definitions are no longer workable if the goal is sustainability in a world of webs and networks and rapid changes. The governance organization must manifest a systemic model of sustainability. If operated in an interactive, interdependent and coordinated way, then continuous success can be expected. Digital electronics give us the tools for quick information, networking, and assessments in order to manage this extra degree of complexity.

- **Planning for the long term and governing strategically.** More front-loaded investment in the development of valid measures of success, evaluative studies of best practices, and outlines and deliberations of alternatives will lead to better plans. Government must develop the will to support the shared plans, to commit to transparent data collection, updating procedures, and administering the plans and policies through attention to fine-grain strategic plans. Policy makers and government leaders need the knowledge and courage to support good planning. The public must insist on such knowledge and courage in the bodies of government staff as well as community political leadership.

- **Commitment, continuity, and monitoring.** The governance structure needs to be organized to assure the citizens of government's commitment to the shared plans of the public and private sectors and existence of continuity in the plan, review, approval, and implementation stages. Additionally, one of the newest characteristics of planning for sustainability is the maintenance of a system of monitoring, measurements, or indicators—in other words, knowing when there is progress or regression from the plan. The U.N. Development Program, for example, recommends a formula-driven city development index that calculates infrastructure (water, sewage, electricity, and telephone connections), waste (wastewater and solid waste treated and disposed), health (life expectancy and child mortality rates), education (literacy and school enrollments), and economic city product (gross domestic product) to measure the city's progress among key indicators from time to time.[62] For the goal of true sustainability, however, a more complex system of sustainability indicators is required. As an example, see the "Five Domains of Sustainability Indicators from an Urban Neighborhood" (page 67) developed to aid growth management in a multiple-communities and multiple-counties region.[63]

- **Urban design as image-making and aid to strategic governance.** Planning and development communications are difficult to transmit among and between interested parties and stakeholders. Three-dimensional images of proposed urban environments become critical to good understanding of the impacts and complexities of most proposals. Urban design, which clearly articulates images and representations of unbuilt urban environments within the built context of the city, are enormous aids to understanding and education. Urban design studies should also be a regular palette of the decision-making mechanisms and the

Five Domains of Sustainability Indicators for an Urban Neighborhood

Environmental Indicators

- Best solar site orientation for all buildings
- Landscaping/heat dissipation/green space
- Community gardens
- Energy efficiency/alternative sources
- Materials recycling/reuse

Socio-Cultural Indicators

- Promotion and facilities for active lifestyles
- Proximity of schools; community partnerships
- Street, public safety
- Adequate, convenient health services
- Mixed ethnic populations/incomes/ages/genders/sexual preferences
- Mixed land uses; convenience and proximity of daily needs
- Active neighborhood association

Technological Indicators

- Choices of efficient, affordable transportation
- Adequate, maintained public infrastructure
- Access to digital communications services
- Efficient, affordable energy systems/distributed generation systems

Economic Indicators

- Public/private partnerships for new/infill development
- Stable to rising property values
- Neighborhood entrepreneurship/local ownership
- Low vacancy rates for housing/commercial properties

Public Policy Indicators

- An up-to-date district or neighborhood comprehensive plan
- Participatory government
- Building codes that emphasize performance standards
- Design guidelines for new/rehab developments
- Zoning ordinances that support the five domains
- Public support for historic preservation/conservation
- Public support for a municipal green building program
- Local recycling, public waste reduction policies

communications for strategic thinking about the qualities and futures of districts and neighborhoods within the city governance.

- **Willingness to look at boundaries, districts, and edges in new ways.** Because principles of sustainability call, on the one hand, for the definition of problems by manageable scope—not by isolation of single elements but by comprehension of integrated systems—and on the other hand, for understanding the larger linkages and external influences, there is a new need to look at the city simultaneously in both polynucleated (villages, districts, and neighborhoods) forms and functions as well as regional and global connections. We must do a better job of anticipating the consequences of our actions and the edge effects of each plan.

  The city of Toronto, Canada, is a good example of a best practice for polynucleated planning and zoning. The urban plan of Toronto is one of the rare comprehensive plans that promotes and encourages cultural districts. While most U.S. comprehensive plans seek to prohibit ethnic enclaves, Toronto planning is based on the belief that strong neighborhoods with common ethnic backgrounds encourage districts of common ethnicity. The rich tapestry of ethnic businesses, cultural celebrations of food heritages, strong schools with common goals and performance standards, and common spiritual and work ethic relationships create a more interesting, creative city with authentic freedoms for the city's citizens than the amalgamated common planning and zoning theory in the United States.

- **Green building programs and the LEED criteria.**[64] Green building is one of many strategies for achieving the goal of sustainable communities. A program in Scottsdale, Ariz., provides the clearest definition for this strategy. It describes green building as "a whole systems approach utilizing design and building techniques to minimize environmental impact and reduce the energy consumption of a building while contributing to the health of its occupants."

Over the past decade, green building ideas have inspired multiple efforts with national, regional, state, and local focal points. As programs developed, ideas about green building were founded based on technical insights and applicability to unique situations. Although the proliferation of the concept is a good thing, the dense and incompatible nature of the programs requires significant sifting for the establishment of second-generation programs.

Applying green building principles requires a contextual model for considering integration of sustainability factors associated with community. These basic factors include environment, economics, socio-cultural elements, public policy, and technology. Simplified, each basic factor represents an ideologically different way for people to relate within a defined area, called the community. But as all who live in communities have experienced, it is the complexity and integration of these factors that create the sense of place. For long-term success, implementing a green building program will require attention to each factor and the interdependent complexities inherent in the community. A systematic approach with emphasis on facilitating education, visioning, and participation is the best way to build sustainable communities.

One system of green building metrics, the Leadership in Energy and Environmental Design (LEED) rating system, created by and maintained through the nonprofit U.S. Green Building Council, is having a major influence on the green characteristics of new construction across the United States as well as other nations. A system of planning, design, and construction checklists has been formalized for projects seeking the LEED certification. Within any community-adopted green building program, the LEED criteria should be considered a minimum standard for green buildings, and the criteria should be correlated with the broader community standards for the five domains of sustainability. If the United States is to achieve the international target reductions of global carbon emissions demanded by the international conferences on global warming, then the minimum standards will not suffice. The categories and credit checklists promoted by the LEED standards are:

Planning sustainable sites
- Landscaping for erosion control
- Landscaping/exterior design to reduce heat islands
- Infill development
- Reduced habitat disturbance
- Site preservation/restoration
- Efficient building location
- Alternative transportation facilities
- Alternative fueling facilities
- Brownfield development

Improving energy efficiency
- Energy efficiency
- Natural ventilation, heating, cooling
- Waste heat recovery system
- Renewable/alternative energy
- International performance measurement and verification protocol

Conserving materials and resources
- Existing building rehabilitation
- Resource reuse
- Recycled content
- Construction waste management plan
- Use of local materials
- Elimination of CFCs, HCFCs, halons
- Occupant recycling

Enhancing indoor environmental quality
- Construction IAQ management plan
- Use of Low VOC materials

- Permanent air monitoring system
- Design of chemical storage areas
- Architectural entryways

Safeguarding water

- Water-conserving fixtures
- Water recovery system
- Water-conserving cooling towers
- Water efficient landscaping
- Surface runoff filtration
- Surface runoff reduction
- Biological waste treatment
- International performance measurement and verification protocol

Improving the design process

- Use of LEED-accredited designer(s)

- **Education, awareness, and engagement.** The pace of change, the intensities of human expectations, and the restriction of natural, economic, and skilled human resources places more pressure than ever before on each city to be a sustained learning community. An enlightened, aware, and knowledgeable citizenry will be willing and able partners in the planning and governance of a healthy, sustainable community. A new commitment by government and urban educational institutions to lifelong and adult education is essential to the planning process for sustainability.

Our society's objective for the lifestyles of future generations should not necessarily be the reduction of consumption but the reduction of the consumption of nonrenewable resources. However, this goal requires a new conservation-based ethic and new practice methodologies for the way we make goods, places, and products. A pervasive EcoSTEP^SM strategy for sustainable design, planning, and urban administration can result in a balance of the five domains and thus real sustainability.

CHAPTER 7

A Biologic Systems View*
as Guidance to the Five
Domains Theory

I n his seminal writings, physicist and systems theorist Fritjof Capra leads the lay reader from an understanding of cell biology and its growth and development processes as the basic foundation of all living systems through the evidence of conditions of cognition and social interactions within all levels and elements of living systems.[65] He exposes intriguing comparisons and relationships between the biological science of living systems and contemporary technologies, cultures, business organizations, and social systems. For instance, he writes, "In biology, the behavior of a living organism is shaped by its structure. As the structure changes (and they all do, constantly) during the organism's development and during the evolution of its species, so does its behavior. A similar dynamic can be observed in social systems. The biological structure of an organism corresponds to the material infrastructure of a society, which embodies the society's culture. As the culture evolves, so does its infrastructure—they co-evolve through continual mutual influences."

Not only are his comparisons and metaphors from science important to today's community issues of culture, structure, consumption of resources, and social organizations, but he also provides challenges for new

*The Hidden Connections: Integrating the Biological, Cognitive, and Social Dimensions of Life Into A Science of Sustainability, Fritjof Capra, Doubleday, 2002. Capra has written two additional important books challenging the reductionist and linear thinking of much of modern science: The Tao of Physics and The Web of Life.

process and knowledge foundations of design and technologies through which we could achieve higher levels of sustainability for our communities and human habitations. Design, "ecodesign" he says, should be modeled from the dynamic processes of nature's ecosystems, which are sustainable communities of plants, animals, and microorganisms. A sustainable human community, he says, "is one designed in such a manner that its way of life, businesses, economy, physical structures, and technologies do not interfere with nature's inherent ability to sustain life."

The first step in our endeavor to build sustainable communities, according to Capra, must be to become "ecologically literate" (i.e., "to understand the principles of organization, common to all living systems, that ecosystems have evolved to sustain the web of life"). Such understandings, he believes, will "become a critical skill for politicians, business leaders, and professionals in all spheres, and should be the most important part of education at all levels—from primary and secondary schools to colleges, universities, and the continuing education and training of professionals." The foundation which he recommends for "ecoliteracy" consists of six principles of ecology:

- **Networks.** At all scales of nature, we find living systems nesting within other living systems—networks within networks. Their boundaries are not boundaries of separation but boundaries of identity. All living systems communicate with one another and share resources across their boundaries.

- **Cycles.** All living organisms must feed on continual flows of matter and energy from their environment to stay alive, and all living organisms continually produce waste. However, an ecosystem generates no net waste, one species' waste being another species' food. Thus, matter cycles continually through the web of life.

- **Solar energy.** Solar energy, transformed into chemical energy by the photosynthesis of green plants, drives the ecological cycles.

- **Partnership.** The exchanges of energy and resources in an ecosystem are sustained by pervasive cooperation. Life did not take over the planet by combat but by cooperation, partnership, and networking.

- **Diversity.** Ecosystems achieve stability and resilience through the richness and complexity of their ecological webs. The greater their biodiversity, the more resilient they will be.

- **Dynamic balance.** An ecosystem is a flexible, ever-fluctuating network. Its flexibility is a consequence of multiple feedback loops that keep the system in a state of dynamic balance. No single variable is maximized; all variables fluctuate around their optimal values.

Connections—in our thinking, our knowledge and information systems, within and among our organizations, by and between the systems we design, and between our constructed infrastructures and buildings and the people and cultures in our communities, with no net waste --are the ecological sustainability goals worthy of our efforts to create sustainable communities. Some of us, Capra included, believe that a decisive number of people have begun a transition to ecological sustainability.

Transferring the Biologic Model to Construction

Capra makes the point that all of life, even the basic cell, is interconnected, responds to its environment, is intelligent, communicates, thrives within diversity, and generates no net waste—except for humans.

The construction and development process of sheltering and accommodating our human needs and activities is singularly the most wasteful process we conduct, at least in times of peace among us.

There are constants, some of which we have ignored at our peril. The evolution of human needs and desires seems insatiable; technologies, institutions, and policies of governance are constantly changing; nothing made of natural materials and substances is free from decay as all natural materials grow, evolve, change, and decay; all energy is solar-based (and free); and all living systems are interconnected and dependent on each other for sustained life.

It seems that we have arrived at a time when building and construction plans and decisions must recognize, in a more deliberate and effective way, these constants, and in a more life-like way create a successful fusion among the five key conditions of any sustainable development. First, our efforts must exhibit a greater environmental sensitivity. Second, real attention must be paid to human and cultural well-being. Third, a life cycle quest for resource and technological efficiency must be planned. Fourth, our projects must be financially feasible, both initially and over the life of the construction. And fifth, we must pay greater attention to the interdependence between good development and good public policies.

When we recognize the full implications of such connections, interconnections, and fusion strategies, a much greater burden is placed on the design process than has been the custom. Where design schools, since early in the industrial revolution, have taught the search for a concept, or a form of expression, we should now see teaching that demands integrative strategies or interdependent, evolutionary dynamics, as the key language of design. Regardless of semantics, the challenges of designing, planning, and making communities sustainable in the 21st century will be these:

- Respect all the natural resources—land, water, air, energy—and all their components.

- Use what is already available (i.e., site/solar orientation, reusable and recycled materials).

- Engage all the stakeholders in the design process. (Maximize teams of experts and stakeholders in the design process from beginning to completion.)

- Use the best performing, least consumptive, and most appropriate technologies. (Learn from others, apply best practices from any and all sources.)

- Relate long-term sustainability objectives to human and natural capital, with economic efficiencies resulting from natural and human efficiencies and through good policies for maintenance, operations, and financing.

- Minimize the embodied energy and the absorbed, nonrenewable energy for construction and operations.

- Make the facility a net energy production center (i.e., designed to produce and distribute more energy than it consumes).

- Design for deconstruction and recycling (or reuse and modification for extended life of materials and facilities).

In the words of Ken Yeang, an award-winning eco-architect in Kuala Lumpur, the design process will need to be transformed into an interdependent process that marshals "whole systems thinking, gives much greater emphasis to the front-loading of design in the process, considers the end-use-least-cost (life-cycle) strategies, and facilitates a team of design minds."[66] Under these conditions, buildings and constructions could actually become more connected to the planet's life systems, and they will be of greater value to human uses.

Is it possible to envision a design/build/recycle process that is more connected to the evolutionary process of life than the making of isolated, disconnected, inanimate objects of consumed natural materials?

One such strategy is beginning to emerge from the construction industry—a *circular renewal system.*[67]

In brief, a circular renewal system is a combined sewage treatment, organic garbage disposal, and energy systems approach, now being tested in some hotels and apartment buildings. The components of a circular renewal system for such buildings work like this:

- An internal system captures all organic residues from the building rather than using traditional municipal sewage lines and garbage collection.

- Hygienic storage tanks and bins (with backup capacity) for the bio-materials feed into an anaerobic digester and an ethanol fermenter.

- The resulting methane serves as a fuel supply to building boilers, kitchens, or electricity generating systems. (Part of the methane could supply a fuel cell for electricity generation in order to test inclusion of this technology as it evolves to cost-competitive commercial operations.)

- The resulting ethanol provides fuel for vehicles for the building operations or possibly for electricity generation.

- Solid residues from the processing are used as compost and fertilizer for the building's landscaping/gardening.

- Liquid effluents from the system are treated and used on site as graywater, reducing overall water demand for the building.

- Supplemental external power may be derived on site from wind generators, photovoltaic systems, or solar water heaters on the roof or other faces of the building envelope, depending on the climate.

These operating systems, combined with successful design strategies for passive cooling/heating, maximization of daylighting along with other energy control systems, and the careful choice of materials for recycled and low-energy content, together give such buildings a distinct biosystems characteristic. They pose the real prospect of recovering the cost of construction in energy savings over the life of the building, of reducing the burden on municipal infrastructures, of reducing the environmental burdens on existing infrastructures from new construction, and coincidentally, of having increased market appeal because the building is a model of environmental excellence.

At least two buildings with similar systems have been constructed in international locations: a hotel in India and a commercial building in Tokyo.

The above examples also highlight the disconnect between what we humans place on Earth for our habitat and accommodations and that which nature supplies, grows, and recycles. (While also observing, through the biological sciences, that different natural systems have interdependencies among each other for the supply and consumption of waste as a part of the web of life.)

The clearest and most dramatic evidence of the disconnection is the volume and frequency of waste from construction and building demolition enterprises. The majority of the materials used and discarded through construction and demolition find no useful secondary or residual purpose, mostly ending up in community landfills. Thus, the construction industry in America is contributing to one of the largest environmental problems we have—landfills that pose threats to human health, the environment, and community landscapes—not to mention the loss of economic value of the waste. Typically, construction and demolition debris accounts for 15 percent to 20 percent of municipal solid waste in the landfills. In some high-growth communities, the volume of this waste may account for 40 percent of the total handled.

At the present time, there are few choices and less incentive for building owners, contractors, designers, or communities to encourage the recycling of construction waste or used building materials back into the local economy. Happily, for the future health of both people and the environment, it does seem that the industry and communities are at the cusp of change. A growing number of nonprofit, for-profit, and government-sponsored organizations are showing up, principally in large urban communities, and in the most environmentally active communities, to bring order and conservation to this imbalance. There were more than 135 representatives of organizations, municipalities, and industries in attendance in 2006 at the University of Florida's International Conference on Deconstruction and Materials Reuse.

Not surprisingly, because of its other progressive policies for growth management and sustainable communities, the Portland, Ore., metro-

politan region is one of the leaders in thinking about policies and practices for construction and demolition waste. As an aid to the industry, the
Metro organization (www.metro-region.org) has published the "Metro
Construction Industry Recycling Toolkit,"[68] for architects, designers,
specification writers, developers, property owners, property managers,
and construction project managers.

With a goal of preventing waste from construction activities, the
Toolkit provides sample record-keeping forms and detailed model in-
structions. It advises:

- Set waste prevention goals and include them in specifications.

- Require specific waste prevention activities in the waste management plan, including reuse and salvage practices.

- Design with standard sizes for all building materials.

- Specify green building materials such as certified wood or low
  VOC paint.

- Specify materials and assemblies that can be easily disassembled at
  the end of their useful life (design for deconstruction).

- Choose flexible interior finishes or materials, such as carpet tiles,
  that can be easily removed and recycled and replaced when worn
  or damaged.

- Design spaces to be flexible for and adaptable to changing uses.

- Communicate your waste prevention plan at meetings, post it at
  the job site, monitor the program, and promote the results.

- Require vendors to ship materials to the job site in recyclable or
  reusable packaging.

- Re-evaluate estimating procedures to make sure the correct amount
  of each material is delivered to the site.

- Maintain an up-to-date material ordering and delivery schedule to minimize the amount of time the materials are on site and to reduce the chance of damage.

- Ask suppliers to deliver supplies using sturdy, returnable pallets and containers. Have them pick up the empty containers when delivering new supplies. Also require suppliers to take back or buy back substandard, rejected, or unused items.

With a goal of saving materials from demolition activities, the Toolkit offers the following guidance: "There are two ways to recover materials for salvage and reuse: Deconstruct the building or conduct a selective salvage operation prior to demolition. Deconstruction involves the careful dismantling of a whole structure in reverse order of assembly, usually by hand, to re-harvest materials for reuse. Salvage is the removal of certain valuable reusable building materials before demolition."

Recycling and Reuse of Building Materials

An example of a construction and demolition salvage alternative is EcoStores Nebraska in Lincoln, Neb. It provides a place where materials can be donated rather than landfilled, selling second-use building and remodeling materials to the public at 50 percent to 90 percent off new retail prices.[69] As a business component of the Joslyn Institute for Sustainable Communities, it accepts tax-deductible donations of almost any usable building or remodeling material. Many sizes and types of windows, tile, brick, stone, roofing, cabinets, toilets, bathtubs, doors, and wood flooring, trim, and lumber are among the typical donations.

EcoStores Nebraska and its companion operation, DeConstruction Nebraska, provide the city of Lincoln with a unique and much-needed opportunity to address the serious issue of construction and demolition waste and its effects on the environment by keeping usable items out of the landfill and the larger waste stream.

Conventional building and remodeling practices use many natural resources, and the standard construction process creates considerable waste. In fact, debris from building construction, renovation, and demolition accounts for nearly 40 percent of the materials disposed in our landfills (nationally, an average of 2.8 pounds per person per day). This debris is composed of excess building materials that contain valuable, often nonrenewable resources and embodied energy from their production and transportation to the job site. Once materials have been consigned to landfills, these resources are virtually impossible to recover.

As much as 8,000 pounds of waste are typically thrown into a landfill during the construction of a single 2,000-square-foot home. In addition to increasing the burden on landfill capacity and operation this represents, waste from paints, solvents, and chemically treated wood can cause soil and water pollution. Additionally, the embodied energy originally used to produce these materials—both by nature and by human processes—is wasted when materials end up in the landfill.

Reusing and recycling materials, on the other hand, extends local landfill life, preserves natural resources, reduces pollution, and saves energy.

From this and other information now becoming available, one can envision a new and major influence on practices and the public policy environment for the construction industry. These changes will perhaps bring us closer to the interdependency model of nature—design for sustainability and the reuse of natural materials. Through the influence of the USGBC LEED standards, emerging national municipal green building programs, and the economic and social pressures for greater energy efficiencies in construction (especially in housing markets) we are beginning to see some important new innovations and best practices. But how do we know these experiments are truly good practices, let alone best practices? Case studies tell us much about the applications of new technologies, new practices, and how we can measure the efficiencies of such practices and applications.

CHAPTER 8

Use of the EcoSTEP^{SM} Tool for Comparisons of Similar Buildings

The Joslyn Institute has conducted a case study of comparable sustainability conditions for three recently constructed net zero energy homes in the Omaha/Lincoln metro area of Nebraska.[70] One home was constructed as part of a green homes development by a commercial development company, one was constructed as a research project by faculty and students at the University of Nebraska-Omaha, and one was constructed by faculty and students from the College of Architecture at the University of Nebraska-Lincoln. Net zero has become a common definition for a construction that is intended to use less energy than the building and its systems will use for the home's own maintenance and operation (i.e., flow-through energy consumption). (Technically, a truly net zero condition in construction would not exist unless all of the embodied and applied energy for the placement of materials in the construction could also be calculated.)

Archspace | 631 North 24th Street, Lincoln, Neb.

Archspace is located in the Malone neighborhood of Lincoln within five blocks of four different bus routes that give users access to all other bus routes in the city.

The Malone neighborhood is an older neighborhood covering 0.546 square miles. The median age of residents in the neighborhood is 29.2 years, and the average household size is 2.2 people. The average estimated value of detached houses in 2007 was $100,441. The percentage of the population in the Malone neighborhood below the poverty level is 37.2 percent. Almost 14 percent (13.83 percent) of the homes in the Malone neighborhood have nine or more rooms, and 32.04 percent have three bedrooms.

Archspace is constructed of wood frame construction with drywall interior finish. The exterior finish consists of fibrous concrete siding.

Archspace Stats	
Average quality	
3 bed / 2.5 bath	
Two-story home with one-car detached garage	
Site value	$25,000
Subject market value	$168,006
Total value	$193,006
Lot area	4,700 sq. ft.
Total living area	1,876 sq. ft.
Total finished area	1,876 sq. ft.
Total area	3,059 sq. ft.
Cost per square foot	$89.56

Figures 29, 30. Archspace house

The Madison | 3111 West Covered Bridge Drive, Rural Lincoln, Neb. The Madison is located just outside of the Lincoln city limits, south of the Pester Ridge neighborhood in the Bridges Development. There is no access to public transportation from this location since the closest bus route is 5.22 miles away from the home.

The Bridges Development is a new residential development, and the adjacent Pester Ridge Development is relatively new as well. The follow-

The Madison Stats	
Very good quality	
1 bed (3 incl. basement) / 2.5 bath	
One-story home with one-car attached garage	
Site value	$120,000
Subject market value	$476,365
Total value	$596,365
Lot area	20,899 sq. ft.
Total living area	1,847 sq. ft.
Total finished area	3,376 sq. ft.
Total area	3,376 sq. ft.
Cost per square foot	$141.10

© April Kick

© April Kick

Figures 31, 32. The Madison house

ing information is regarding Pester Ridge due to a lack of information about the Bridges, which will have 70 homes in its 181-acre space. The median age of residents in Pester Ridge is 25.9 years, and the average household size is 3.2 people. The estimated value of detached houses in 2007 was $278,491. The percentage of the population in Pester Ridge below the poverty level is 6.8 percent. More than 30 percent (30.54 percent) of the homes in the Pester Ridge neighborhood have nine or more rooms, and 52.16 percent have three bedrooms.

The Madison is wood frame construction with drywall interior finish. The exterior finish consists of stucco and stone veneer.

ZNETH | 6454 Woolworth Avenue, Omaha, Neb.

ZNETH is located in the Aksarben neighborhood in Omaha with a bus route four blocks away that gives access to downtown Omaha, a pedestrian bridge, a medical center, Masonic Manor, Ak-Sar-Ben Village, Bergan Mercy Hospital, and a shopping mall. Along this route there are several transfer points from which users can access multiple bus lines to travel elsewhere in Omaha.

The Aksarben neighborhood is an older neighborhood in Omaha covering 1.547 square miles. The median age of residents is 33.5 years, and the average household size is 2.2 people. The average estimated value of detached houses in 2007 was $115, 504. The percentage of the population in the Aksarben neighborhood below the poverty level is 10.6 percent. Less than 5 percent (4.85 percent) of the homes in the Aksarben neighborhood have nine or more rooms, and 43.09 percent have three bedrooms.

The ZNETH is wood frame construction, ground-level ICF walls, with drywall interior finish. The exterior finish is stucco.

ZNETH Stats

Average quality

2 bed (4 incl. basement) / 2.5 bath

Two-story home with one-car detached garage

Site value	$12,500
Improvement	$73,200
(based on below statement estimate $237,500)	
Total value	$85,700
($250,000 was the estimate given)	
Lot area	5,940 sq. ft.
Total living area	2,232 sq. ft.
Total finished area	3,640 sq. ft. (est.)
Total area	3,640 sq. ft. (est.)
Cost per square foot	$20.11 ($65.25)

© April Kick

© April Kick

Figures 33, 34. ZNETH house

The Joslyn Institute for Sustainable Communities developed the following list of 20 sustainability indicators for comparative purposes among the three constructions:

Environmental Domain
- Sustainable material use: second-use materials and recycled material
- Water conservation practices
- Reduction of carbon emissions
- Landscape enhancement

Socio-Cultural Domain
- Teaching environment
- Public impact and influence on the neighborhood
- Site impact
- Recycling practices

Technological Domain
- Low-tech natural systems
- Energy conservation systems and updating
- Planning for alternate transportation
- Use of alternate energy sources

Economic Domain
- Use of existing infrastructure
- Affordability
- Return on investment / cost benefit analysis
- Energy monitoring and adjustment

Public Policy Domain
- Alternate sources of energy policy
- Impact on policies regarding water conservation
- Impact on the construction industries
- Intent of impacting residential construction

When these indicators are plotted on the EcoSTEP℠ diagram, the tool reflects the comparative performance of each project against common indicators. In view of the facts that each project was constructed in a common time frame and each has specific systems monitoring technologies built in for long-term evaluations, the following baseline performance information will be useful to set the format for continuing performance evaluations over future years for these pioneering and unique properties. Subsequently, this information will be instructive to new designs for energy efficiencies, and the EcoSTEP℠ tool will become a part of the design briefs.

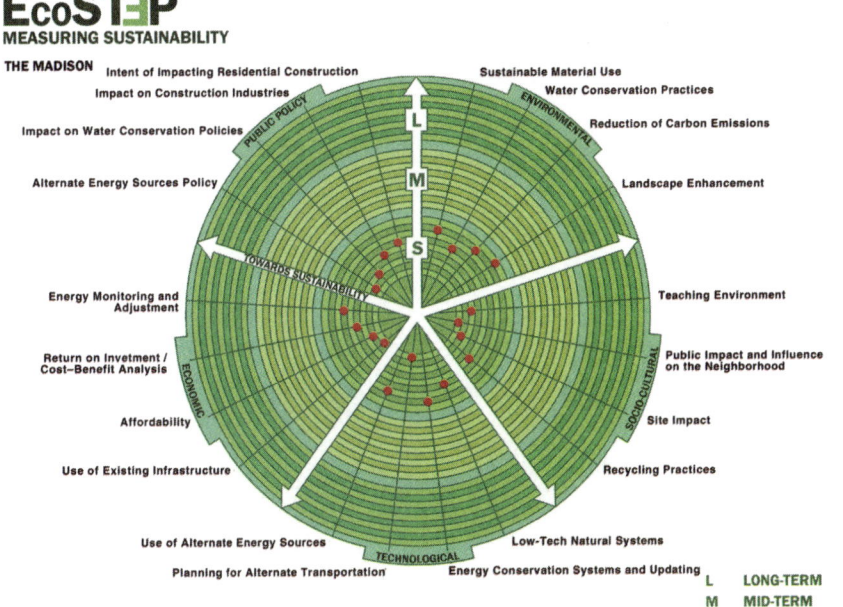

Figure 35. Sustainability measure of the Madison

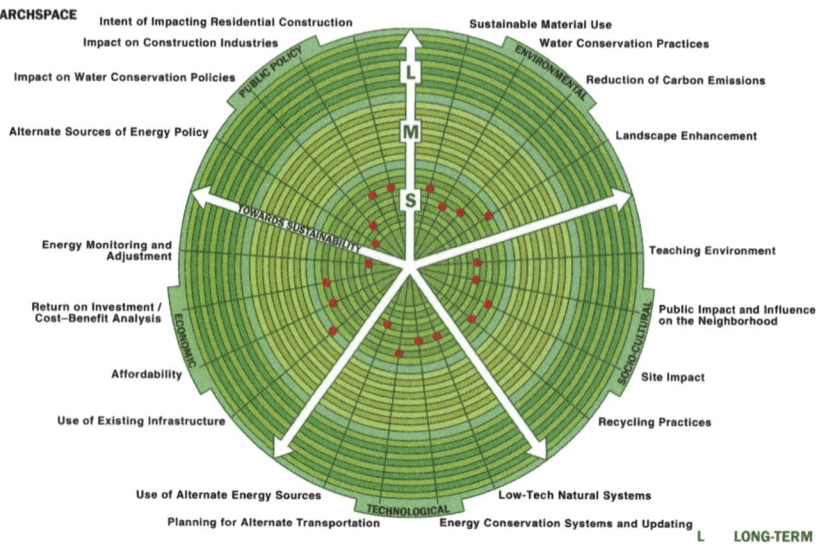

Figure 36. Sustainability measure of Archspace

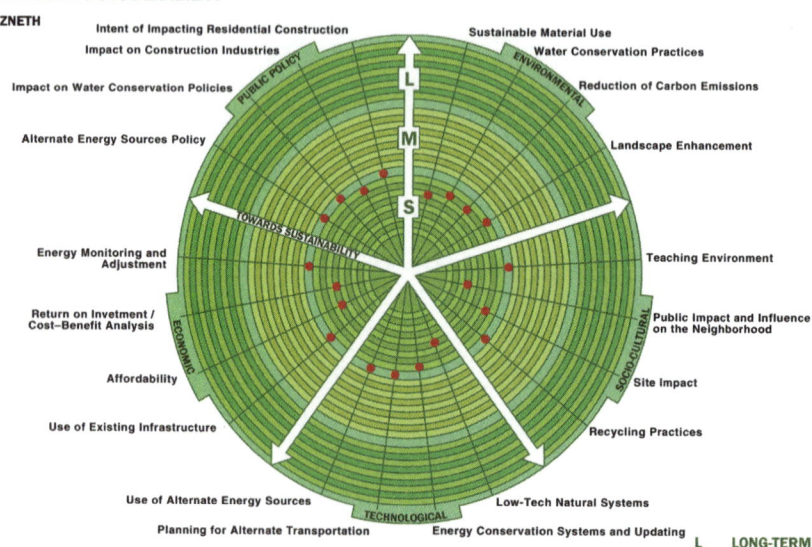

Figure 37. Sustainability measure of ZNETH

Comparative Construction Information on the Three Houses

Using the EcoSTEP℠ tool and the common sustainability indicators, the assessment results in the following comparative information.

Environmental Domain

- All three homes use a significant amount of recycled materials, with the Madison using the most. Nearly every surface in the home consists of recycled materials.

- Both the Madison and Archspace are fitted with low-flow fixtures, and the Madison features dual flush water closets. All three also use rainwater catchments. ZNETH will also feature a greywater system after conventional water use for one year to establish a baseline. However, the Madison is built in a subdivision that includes six man-made ponds.

- Considerable effort was made to reduce the carbon footprint of all three homes. The alternative energies employed at the ZNETH and Madison sites dramatically decrease their carbon footprints. Although Archspace uses alternative energy, it does not do so to the same extent as the other two.

- All three of the homes set a specific goal to include drought resistant plants in their landscaping. In addition, the designers planned to have them watered using collected rainwater.

Socio-Cultural Domain

- Publicity is a large part of creating a teaching environment. With more publicity, ZNETH has extended its teaching environment beyond users and neighbors. In addition, ZNETH will also have more users over its life than the other homes. The Madison intends to educate a select few, namely those living in the small community. On the other hand, students will live in ZNETH. They will conduct tours for anyone, use the home as a laboratory, conduct research based on its systems, and survey the occupants after living in the unique conditions. Students did not have any interaction with the Madison during its design or construction; local learning communities had extensive contact with the other two homes. However, ZNETH will continue to be a teaching environment to new students while the other two homes will become dormant teaching environments as time progresses.

- All the homes are designed to blend into their respective neighborhoods and therefore attract the demographic living in that specific area. The public has had considerably more contact with ZNETH than the other homes. Information about the house in Omaha (ZNETH) is also more readily available than for the other two homes in Lincoln. However, it seems that neighbors had the most interaction with Archspace during its construction.

- Both ZNETH and Archspace were built on infill lots near the city centers of Omaha and Lincoln, respectively. The Madison is built in a new development on the edge of Lincoln. Given this information, ZNETH and Archspace have considerably smaller site impact. In addition to the land used to build the Madison, the rest of the development has also been significantly impacted by the construction of man-made ponds as well as the insertion of necessary infrastructure, utilities, and other residences.

- Part of the construction focus for ZNETH was to reduce waste and recycle all waste that could possibly be recycled. The objective was to send as little to the landfill as possible, to the extent that excess concrete was buried on site. Construction recycling practices were carried out at both of the other homes but not to the extent that was seen at ZNETH.

Technological Domain
- All the homes employ low-tech natural systems, but all still require HVAC systems as well as electric utilities.

- All three homes include Energy Star appliances, and none of them include incandescent lighting. ZNETH has been designed for updating, while the other two have not. Both the Madison and ZNETH use energy recovery ventilation systems, which are the most up-to-date HVAC systems on the market. All three homes are well insulated to avoid unintentional heat loss or gain. The largest difference among the homes is that ZNETH is currently insulated using multiple techniques in order to determine the best choice; in addition, systems and materials will be updated as new products are available to be tested.

- Alternate transportation was a major issue in choosing the sites for ZNETH and Archspace, while alternative transportation seems to have not been considered with regard to the Madison.

- ZNETH is equipped with geothermal heating, cooling, and a tank-less water heater, as well as PVLs and a vertical axis wind turbine. The Madison is equipped with PV panels, a geothermal system, and a geothermal water heater. Archspace has two wind turbines and a geothermal system. ZNETH and the Madison should pro-duce more energy than they will consume and consequently sell energy back to the grid. The geothermal system for the Madison was designed to use the man-made ponds while ZNETH and Arch-space use the ground. Archspace will not produce enough energy to support itself.

Economic Domain

- ZNETH and Archspace relied solely on the existing infrastructures, while the Madison, as part of a new subdevelopment, required that infrastructure be constructed.

- Figures 38 and 39 provide graphical analysis of the costs of the homes.

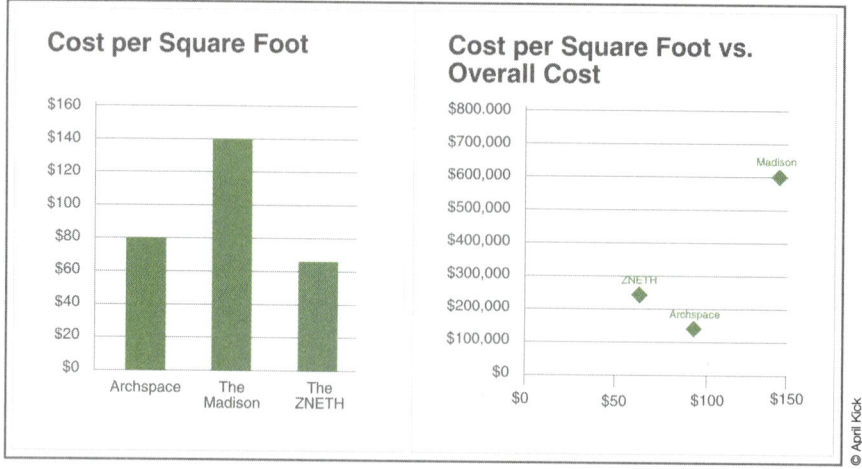

Figure 38. Square foot cost comparisons   Figure 39. Total cost comparisons

- Given the uncertainty of the return on investment and looking strictly at the dollar amounts for the equipment and installation of the alternative energies, a general estimate would assume that Archspace would see a return on investment first and the Madison last.

- Although energy production will be monitored at the Madison and ZNETH, ZNETH's monitoring will be considerably more extensive. Energy, both used and produced, can be adjusted by the users of the ZNETH, while it will only be observed by those at the Madison. Archspace does not have a feature like this.

Public Policy Domain

- There are some public policies that make the use of alternate energy sources or other sustainable practices not possible in residential applications. However, the Omaha project challenged limitations, has held public policy in question, and has in turn changed public policy. On the other hand, the Madison and Archspace projects did not face any of these issues head on.

- The only project that needed to confront public policies regarding water conservation was ZNETH; the others did not need to.

- All three homes came into contact with the construction industries, but ZNETH had some very specific details and complicated systems for which it was necessary to speak with many manufacturers directly as well as work out some unprecedented situations during construction. Rezac Builders, the contractor for the Madison, made less of an impact through exposure and change within its industry. Likewise, it does not seem that the Archspace home made as much of an impact as ZNETH, but it did impact some of the mechanical, electrical, and plumbing contractors that worked on the project.

- All of the projects were undertaken partly to provide an example to everyone that it could be done. However, ZNETH is also to be used as a place to try out new technologies and test materials used in the construction of a home. ZNETH seems to have the largest impact at this point, followed by Archspace. With additional publicity, it is likely that Archspace would have generated more attention than ZNETH due to its lower cost.

CHAPTER 9

Post-Occupancy Evaluation: An Alternative Use of the EcoSTEP^{SM} Tool

I n 1993, W. Cecil Steward converted an existing 97-year-old commercial property into a multi-unit residence. He and his spouse would use one unit, plus there would be two low-income rental apartments. Following the development of the EcoSTEP^{SM} tool, the property was used as a case study for post-occupancy evaluation applications on existing buildings. The following sustainability indicators for existing urban residential properties has been applied to the tool for plotting the success (or failure) of the original retrofit design intentions:

Figures 40, 41, 42, 43, 44. Steward residence retrofit

Steward Residence Indicators

* Key indicators

Environmental Domain

- Influenced green development downtown*
- Influenced green design and construction
- Energy conservation materials*
- Saved 97-year-old building
- Reused and recycled materials
- Demonstrated walkability / conservation of energy*

Socio-Cultural Domain

- Added to arts awareness
- Increased social interaction*
- Community learning through repetitive open house
- Handicap accommodations for elderly parent*
- Added to community low-income housing
- Provided case study teaching environment
- Visible streetscape improvement

Technological Domain

- Global connections / virtual office*
- Use of low-tech natural systems
- Use of environmental context
- Energy conservation systems
- Use of recycle technologies*
- Use of second-use materials
- Added public attention to planning for alternative transportation systems

Economic Domain

- Uses existing infrastructure
- Assistance to low-income with affordable housing*
- Contributed to removal of blight*

- Good return on investment*
- Contribution local economy through employment*
- Public funds leveraged private funds*
- Added to increased tax income to city

Public Policy Domain

- Attention to alternative sources of energy policy
- Researched green building programs
- Influenced the uses of public right of way*
- Influenced downtown revitalization
- Influenced rewrite of comprehensive plan*
- Influenced sub-area downtown master plan*
- Water conservation uses policy

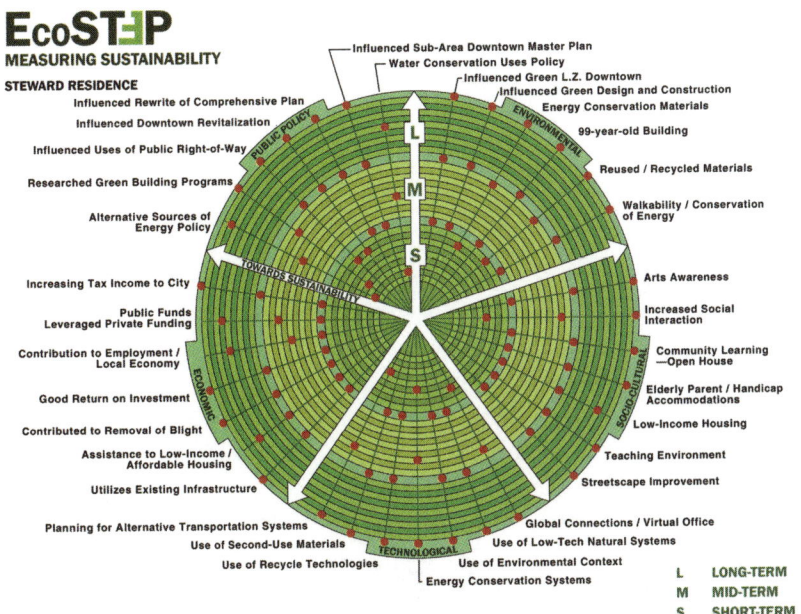

Figure 45. Steward residence post-occupancy evaluation

Conclusion from These Comparisons

Energy efficiency in existing and new buildings is, of course, the most urgent design, planning, and urban administration challenge now and, most likely, for the next 50 years. However, as the preliminary work of the U.N. Economic Commission for Europe (and North America)[71] shows in exquisite detail, the most appropriate and opportune focus for the moment is the housing sector. This contemporary challenge does not mean that the professions, public policy officials, or the public can afford not to give equal and immediate attention to all other aspects of community sustainability. These include environmental conservation and protections for threatened resources and habitats, social equities and cultural heritages, appropriate and affordable technologies, economic sharing that does not overburden future generations, and public policies that facilitate sustainable development throughout the community wherever people and nature's creatures choose to live.

© Lisa F. Young / Fotolia

© Sergiy Serdyuk and Laurent Dambies / Fotolia and Diane Wanek / Zigzag Design

CHAPTER 10

Sustainometrics Relationships and Values

To know whether we are giving adequate, holistic consideration to all of these aspects of community sustainability in the process of deliberation and the making of designs, there is a need for an overarching, defined framework of relationships and values among and between the domains as well as the indicators that may be defined within each domain. While balance among and between the five domains has been stated as an operative goal in seeking sustainable conditions, the universal goal in the practice of sustainable decision making should be developmental decisions that result in conditions of circular, life cycle conservation of natural resources.

Achieving this goal means that the framework of relationships and values must be defined in a manner that will be applicable to all contexts and problem statements. It also means that the process can be standardized—repeatable and replicable—even under new conditions and with dynamic indictors. This is the very reason for the design of the EcoSTEP^{SM} tool.

The logic underlying the tool does not strive for conditions of equal value among the five domains nor for a relationship between every indicator. But it does seek a balance of relationships that will result in the environmental domain having preeminent importance or at least a greater value than the other four. Each of the other four domains has an assigned value that aggregately will support the desired outcome of environmental conservation.

Because the EcoSTEP^{SM} tool demands that each of the domains and indicators within are interdependent and that there are logical differences in value among the domains, the relationships and impacts of one sustainability indicator over any other on the chart can become a matter of complex definitions. Therefore, it is important to assign mathematical values to the domains and indicators.

Figure 48 gives a value of 10 to each of the domains in a perfect state of sustainability. In a negative (declining) state, the following points are assigned:

- The environmental domain is assigned 10 points that are available for reductions among the total indicators in that domain.

- The socio-cultural domain is assigned 4 points.

- The technological domain is assigned 4 points.

- The economic domain is assigned 6 points.

- The public policy domain is assigned 8 points.

These value statements could also be understood as percentage statements of the default 10 that may possibly be changed by the reduction of values of the various indicators. In net effect these variations of point values gives a range of distinctive importance, each domain in relation to the other four. In other words, the variation of values establishes mathematical relationships among and between the several sustainability indicators.

Figure 48 establishes the critical relationships between each of the domains based on practical conditions of successful sustainable development projects.

Figure 49 assigns proportional mathematical values to each of the sustainability indicators according to their appropriate domains (using the previously described indicators for the growth community case study).

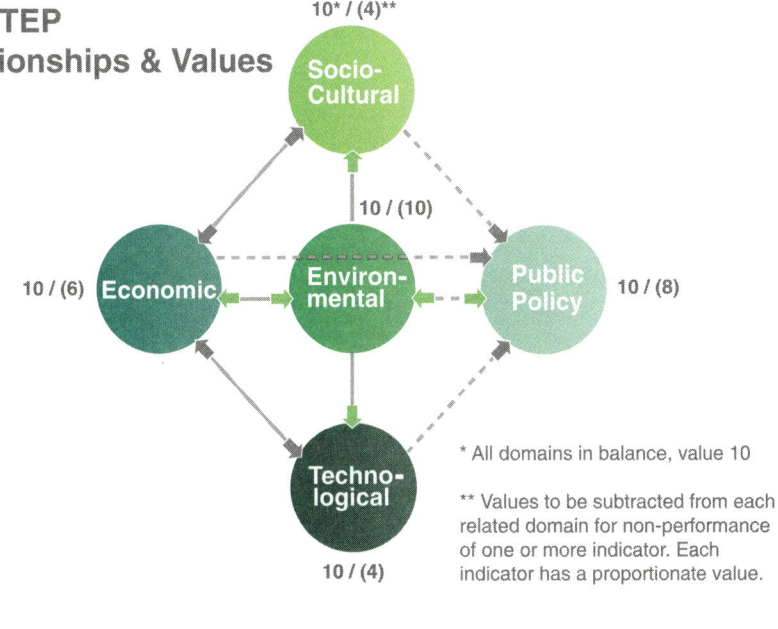

Figure 48. Relationships and values of domains and indicators

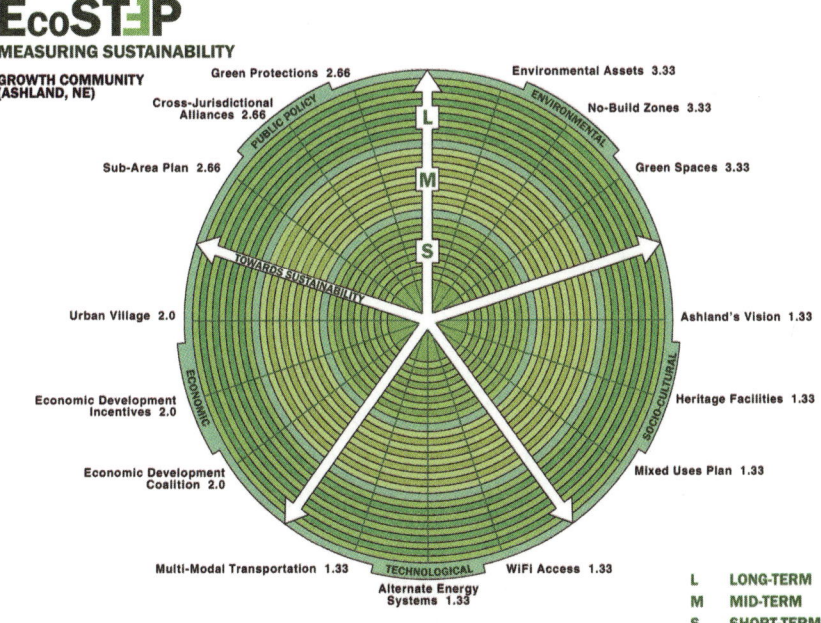

Figure 49. EcoSTEP^{SM} chart with sustainability indicator values

As an example of application of the tool, Figure 50 illustrates a project chart for one of the previously described urban revitalization charrettes, the Drake Court district in Omaha, Neb. In this model, we have assumed that one indicator in the public policy domain and one in the economic domain have made no progress toward a sustainable condition; in other words, there has been a failure by the city to accomplish these indicators (designated by the "XX" on the indicator lines in Figure 51). Thus, the assigned value for each of these indicators is to be deducted from the remaining indicators that have a relationship with the public policy and economic domains. Therefore, the plot points in the chart are revised according to the subtraction of value from the affected indicators.

Specifically, the analog or manual procedure for determining the impacts of negative actions (or non-action) resulting in the change of one or more indicators and impacting the remaining indicators proceeds in the following manner.

1. The most appropriate indicators for each domain are added to the EcoSTEP^SM diagram, remembering that every indicator must be measurable and that the data set must be retrievable and able to be calculated for change over time (Figure 50). The most likely means for the initial identification of the key indicators would be professional judgment, consensus opinions of stakeholders in the project, or surveyed opinions of public/community representatives concerned with the project.

2. Having positioned the sustainability indicators on the radial lines of the EcoSTEP^SM diagram, plot the existing status of each indicator on a scale of 1 to 10 in the short-term scale of the diagram (Figure 50). This example defines an existing urban district in an existing community with an intent to upgrade the district to a sustainable condition over nine years. (If the project diagram is used to represent a new, non-existing project or product, then the short-term scale would be used to identify the expected progress toward

a value of 10 for each indicator in the defined short-term (e.g., one year, two years, three years)

3. The indicator lines are plotted for expected or desired progress toward a condition of sustainability during the mid-term and then during the long-term time frames. In this example of the Drake Court district, the mid-term time frame has been determined to be six years, and the long-term timeframe determined to be nine years from the present. The plotting of progress along indicator lines should be the result of the best available professional and practical judgment for real, expected outcomes of the condition of each indicator.

4. Assume, for the sake of demonstration, that two of the initially defined indicators do not materialize: the sub-area plan indicator in the public policy domain (marked "XX"), and the city incentives in the economic domain (also marked "XX"). (See Figure 51.) The sub-area plan indicator has a predetermined value of 2.66, and the city incentives indicator has a predetermined value of 2.0. In the Figure 48 relationships and values diagram, we have indicated a direct relationship between the public policy and environmental domains. Similarly, we have indicated direct relationships between the economic and environmental domains as well as with the socio-cultural, technological, and public policy domains.

5. These relationships require that the sum of the unaccomplished indicators would be subtracted from the sum total of the indicators in each domain that have established relationships with the negatively affected domain. The plot points are then reduced in value according to the new mathematical value and replotted on the diagram. Therefore, one can see that not accomplishing the sub-area plan and not providing for the financial incentives in the economic domain moves the environmental indicators further away from possible sustainable conditions, as it does the socio-cultural and

technological indicators. Making these interactive dynamics visible emphasizes the interdependent nature of the several sustainability indicators.

6. A next step in the EcoSTEP^{SM} charting process might be the application of graphic representations by use of colors and sizes of the plot points to indicate planned priorities and requirements for urgent action related to specific indicators.

Software is currently under development by the Joslyn Institute that will allow the user to study hypothetical what-if assessments of any changing set of sustainability indicators automatically. In the construct of the software, the user will be able to assign new or different priorities to individual indicators and see the impact such decisions will have on other defined indicators as well as gaining an understanding of the net consequence to each of the five domains. The user will be able to define a graphic representation of actionable priorities and critical objectives on the face of the EcoSTEP^{SM} tool. The software will also allow annual or periodic tracking of the progress of all designated indicators toward a condition of sustainability.

The automation of the sustainometrics tool will facilitate decision making, communications, and measurements about the conservation of our limited and nonrenewable resources. The responsibility for conservation-based consumption can be placed squarely in the laps of those of us who design, plan, and administer the growth and development of built, human-made objects and environments.

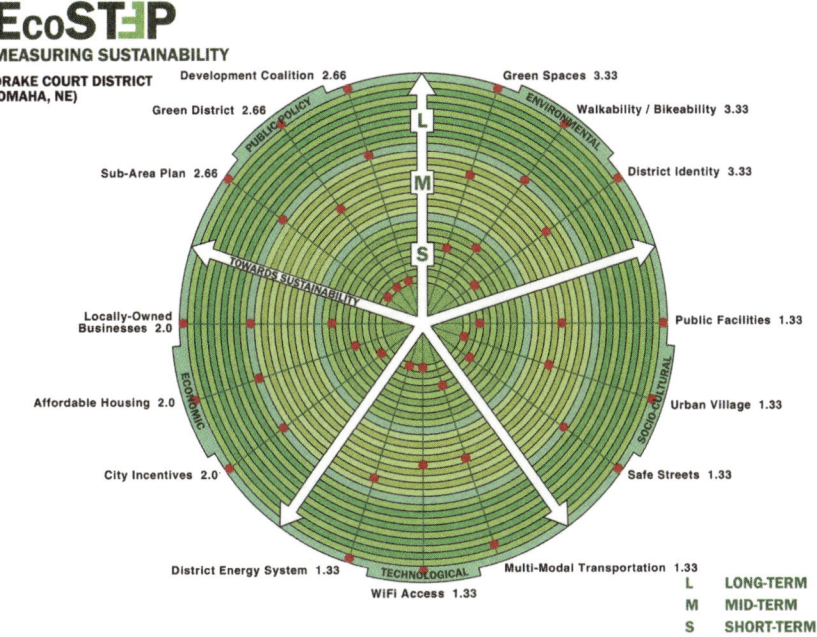

Figure 50. EcoSTEP℠ chart with plotted conditions

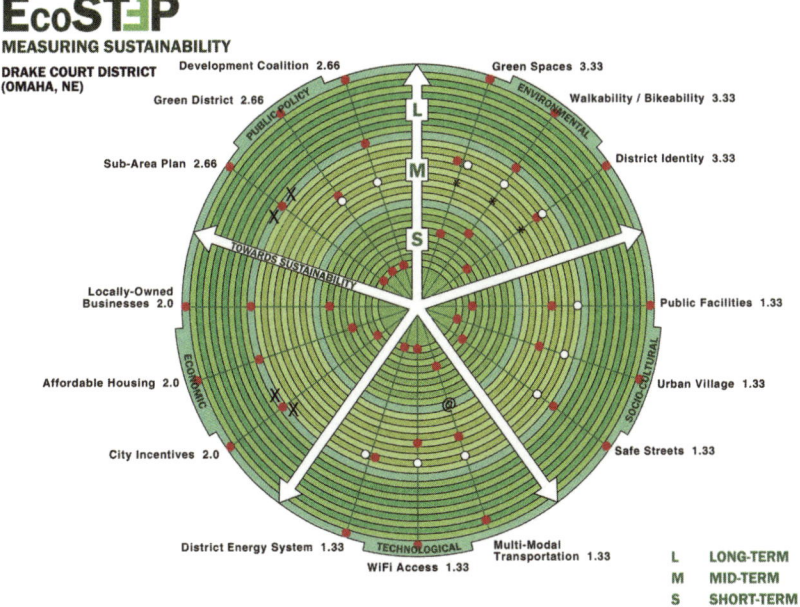

Figure 51. Calculated impact of non-performance and re-charting of indicators

Epilogue

In the beginning of this treatise, three goals were described:

- Assist the reader in understanding the need to consider five domains of sustainability, (in lieu of the original three pillars of sustainability) and their interdependence and interaction upon each other. We have presented examples, a variety of urban and community development models, and evidence of some consequential outcomes by careful consideration of the addition of technological and public policy domains as well as the broadened social domain into socio-cultural. While the five domains foundation is clearly set in the language of development—as contrasted with any intent for preservation of the status quo—we believe we have demonstrated the means toward living and practicing, in our developmental quests, a conservation-based ethic that will sustain both the Earth's natural systems and a diverse human enterprise.

- Distinguish the differences between linear reductionist thinking and the thought process of holistic, interdependent, and interactive analyses for optimal sustainable outcomes. The Western culture is finally, but not uniformly, believing that everything—physically, intellectually, and biologically—is connected to everything else. This system of interactions and interdependencies clearly and distinctly challenges the 19th- and 20th-century framework of straight-line, single-issue Cartesian methods of planning. We have demonstrated that these interactive modes of thinking and planning will result in the best opportunity for dealing with the chaos of the interdependencies and give us the best chance for reducing the number and severity of unintended negative environmental consequences through our human actions.

- Demonstrate the use of the sustainometrics tool EcoSTEP^{SM} metrics for direct application to desired design and planning outcomes (or other sustainability intentions in the built environment) through a range of models, indicators, and project scales and applications. We have presented the theories, organization, and models of applications of sustainometrics through the use of the EcoSTEP^{SM} metrics tool. We also have asserted throughout our deliberations that designers, planners, civic administrators, and community leaders have the primary responsibility for conserving the natural resources of planet Earth. Our corollary responsibilities reside in the context of consumers and consumption of harvested and used resources—products must be made, communities must be designed and planned, and urban and community uses of energy, water, materials, food, and the land are necessities of life. All of these must be created and used in ways that will sustain our finite nonrenewable resources.

Sustainometrics is a new form of measurement of human action in the making of products and the built environment. The systems of thinking and the processes recommended are focused on questions of sustainability—and even survival—of human communities as we know them. Like any existing system of measurement or evaluation (e.g., performance standards, accreditation, LEED building standards, certification programs), we can either accept the standards as maximum objectives, or we can treat the standards as minimum objectives that give us foundations on which to build progress and more creative, conservative solutions for future developments.

History has demonstrated that humans innately seek innovation, new ideas, and alternate ways to enhance the qualities of life. These principles of knowing the impacts of our decisions assume that the quest will continue.

Measurement is critical. It provides something that is essential to sustenance and growth: feedback. All life thrives on feedback and dies without it. We have to know what is going on around us, how our actions impact others, how the environment is changing, and how we're changing. If we don't have access to this information, we can't adapt or grow. Without feedback, we shrivel into routines and develop hard shells that keep newness out. We don't survive for long. In any living system, feedback differs from measurement in several significant ways:

- Feedback is self-generated. Individual and systems notice whatever they determine is important for them. They ignore everything else.

- Feedback depends on context. The critical information is being generated right now. Failing to notice the now or staying stuck in past assumptions is dangerous.

- Feedback changes. What an individual or system chooses to notice will change depending on the past, the present, and the future. Looking for information only within rigid categories leads to blindness, which is also dangerous.

- New and surprising information can get in. The boundaries are permeable.

- Feedback is life-sustaining. It provides essential information about how to maintain one's existence. It also indicates when adaptation and growth are necessary.

- Feedback supports movement toward fitness. Through the constant exchange of feedback, the individual and its environment co-evolve toward mutual sustainability.[72]

Sustainometrics, as both measurement and feedback, will be useful only if we treat the intellectual process as dynamic, malleable in distinct and differing product or place contexts, and participatory among many users and stakeholders.

Design, planning, and decision-making processes about the way we collectively use the natural resources of Earth must respect a conservation ethic for all constructed or human-made products. This ethic will control all decisions about manufacturing, development, construction —the making of human habitats and all of the products and implements used by humans. In such efforts, it is imperative that we know whether we are making sustainable decisions before committing the natural resources to some human use. This *sustainometrics* model, using the EcoSTEP[SM] metrics tool, gives all decision leaders the opportunity for such advanced knowledge, resulting in better, more holistic decision-making.

To know that we are facilitating unsustainable conditions in these domains around the globe in both developed and under-developed habitats means that we (designers, planners, and decision leaders) have a unique responsibility. We must design and plan for sustainable futures, measure current and near-term conditions for progress and future guidance, and have the information and courage to administer as if our and our descendants' lives depended on today's decisions for the long term.

To embrace this responsibility and seek creative, efficient, equitable solutions is to be human. We have only one place to live, but we have many choices about how.

Appendix

Examples of the five domains system of sustainability indicators for selected building types:

Health Care Facilities | Hospitals

Environmental Domain

- Water conservation measures (interior, exterior)
- Stormwater management and landscape practices
- Carbon emissions reduction
- Greenspace/landscape enhancement

Socio-Cultural Domain

- Indoor air quality/healthy environment
- Match quality of patient accommodations with quality of patient care philosophy and practices
- Install green content, recycle, and use waste stream reduction practices for all consumable products

Technological Domain

- Apply on-site alternative energy generation system
- Install energy conservation technologies wherever possible
- Install energy monitoring technologies (see also Economic Domain)

Economic Domain

- Install energy/cost accounting system using monthly energy consumption technology; report system costs quarterly
- Calculate design and installation costs of retrofit technologies and the expected payback schedule for resulting energy savings.

- Calculate economic/environmental cost-benefit conditions for carbon footprint reductions due to phased retrofits.

Public Policy Domain

- Publish a facilities maintenance/operations manual for sustainability for each campus, with specific corporation-wide standards
- Negotiate building and safety policy with the city government and operations and economic impacts with the utility companies for on-site energy generation and conservation measures
- Organize a phased corporation-wide sustainability master plan for retrofit designs and installations

Key considerations when selecting indicators

Environmental

- It is important to reduce the consumption of potable water use for building functions such as sewage conveyance and irrigation so that potable water may be preserved for more critical functions, such as drinking and washing. Water conservation methods should include employing low-flow plumbing fixtures, dual-flush water closets, water-free urinals, efficient dishwashers and laundry washers, and integrated sensors and time stops on faucets and shower heads.

- High-efficiency irrigation systems with moisture sensors should replace the standard time cycle systems now employed. Where possible, rainwater collection or campus greywater systems should be employed to supply irrigation systems.

- Consider changing surface parking lots from impervious material to pervious surface material to reduce rainwater runoff and polluting residue from auto waste. Consider the installation of runoff water cleansing rain gardens on campus sites in natural topography locations to minimize runoff entering community sewer systems. Also consider the installation of rainwater collection and landscape distribution systems at each campus.

- Sustainable landscape practices should include low-emission and energy efficient mechanical maintenance equipment, the installation of low-water and drought-resistant native plants, and the use of grass clippings, leaves, and food waste compost for landscape fertilization in lieu of chemical fertilizers.

- Where the current power supply to facilities is produced primarily by inefficient carbon emissions coal-burning power plants, consider new agreements with the utility companies for a percentage of power supplied by renewable energy sources.

- Consider the installation of on-campus energy generation technologies such as solar-powered photovoltaics or wind energy. As funding becomes available, the increase of both on-site and purchased electricity will be a strategic opportunity.

- Consider a tree planting policy to offset the carbon footprint of the health care campuses. For instance, a tree planted on each hospital campus for each birth delivery at the hospital would be a major metro forestation project and a good public interest project.

Socio-Cultural

- Operational changes for improved indoor comfort can have an added benefit of energy savings, including HVAC nighttime setback in appropriate zones and increasing the campus chilled water supply when the outside air temperature drops. To improve the energy efficiency and the quality of the indoor environment, the corporation should consider the following retrofits:
  - Premium efficiency motor installations when replacement is required
  - Installation of variable frequency devices on all motors over 10 HP
  - Variable air volume systems installation to replace inefficient constant air volume systems to achieve the higher efficiencies.

- Natural light harvesting, conservation of electrical lighting, and the prevention of western and southern façade heat gains through inefficient windows and exterior building thermal shells will increase the comfort of patients and employees for greater patient satisfaction and employee productivity. Building shell and window installations should be accomplished in retrofit phases as funding and modernization planning progresses.

- Consider appointing a corporate supervisor of green teams for each campus. All waste from consumable products and services, including packaging, waste from the use of products, food services, and patient care operations, should be under the purview of the green teams and the corporate green supervisor.

Technological

- The majority of the roof structures of the campus facilities are flat constructions. These locations are ideal for the future installation of solar and wind powered technologies to supply a portion of the off-grid electricity for the campus.

- Employee parking lots provide ideal public awareness opportunities for the installation of photovoltaic systems on parking sheds constructed over portions of the surface lots.

- A regular maintenance cycle of three to five years and replacements to all CFL bulbs is recommended.

- Other recommended technologies: motion/occupancy sensors for light switches in areas that do not have constant occupancy; replace CRT monitors and televisions with LCD; offer low-wattage task lighting in staff locations; replace electric radiant heaters with electric resistance heaters; identify laptops, computers, fax machines, copiers, scanners, water coolers, microwaves, and refrigerators that are not Energy Star rated and replace them accordingly.

- Consider appointment of a green and sustainable systems coordinator for each campus to oversee the reduction of energy consumption through occupant education programs, demand-side management practices, metering, energy-saving improvements to buildings, energy audits, and energy reduction programs. The coordinator could also oversee waste management programs, green purchasing, and staff green teams on each campus.

- Each building should have independent metering and monthly consumption metering, and accounting for electrical, gas, chilled water, potable water, greywater (if any), and rainwater recovery and use.

- An infrastructure for real-time monitoring of energy and water usage at all the major campuses should be developed and tied into a central automated control center.

Economic

- The recommended new and retrofit technologies and renewable sources of energy will bring lower operating costs and sources of new revenue to the health care facilities.

Public Policy

- Ultimately, each campus should have a carbon footprint audit as an adjunct to the sustainability master plan.

- All municipal and state policies related to the infrastructure and operations of the health care delivery facilities should be reviewed for conflicts and barriers to the energy efficiency and conservation-based goals of the corporation.

Housing | Urban Residence/Retrofit of Commercial Building

* Indicators deemed to be of higher priority or value than others in each domain

Environmental Domain

- Influenced green landscape downtown*
- Influenced green design and construction
- Energy conservation materials*
- Saves existing building
- Reused and recycled materials
- Walkability / conservation of energy*

Socio-Cultural Domain

- Arts awareness
- Increased social interaction*
- Community learning through an open house
- Handicap accommodations for elderly*
- Low-income housing
- Teaching environment
- Streetscape improvement

Technological Domain

- Global connections / virtual office*
- Use of low-tech natural systems
- Use of environmental context
- Energy conservation systems
- Use of recycling technologies*
- Use of second-use materials
- Planning for alternative transportation systems

Economic Domain

- Uses existing infrastructure
- Assistance to low-income through affordable housing*
- Contributed to removal of blight*
- Good return on investment*
- Contribution to the local economy through employment*
- Public funds leveraged private funding*
- Increasing tax income to city

Public Policy Domain

- Alternative sources of energy policy
- Researched green building programs
- Influenced the uses of public right of way*
- Influenced downtown revitalization
- Influenced rewrite of comprehensive plan*
- Influenced sub-area downtown master plan*
- Water conservation uses policy

Housing I Energy Efficient Housing/New Construction

Environmental Domain
- Sustainable material use: second-use and recycled materials
- Water conservation practices
- Reduction of carbon emissions
- Landscape enhancement

Socio-Cultural Domain
- Teaching environment
- Public impact and influence on the neighborhood
- Site impact
- Recycling practices

Technological Domain
- Low-tech natural systems
- Energy conservation systems and updating
- Planning for alternate transportation
- Use of alternate energy sources

Economic Domain
- Use of existing infrastructure
- Affordability
- Return on investment / cost-benefit analysis
- Energy monitoring and adjustment

Public Policy Domain
- Alternate sources of energy policy
- Impact on policies regarding water conservation
- Impact on the construction industries
- Intent of impacting residential construction

Housing | Regional Energy Efficient Housing

Environmental Domain

- Maximize the ecological benefits of the climatic context
- Minimize the use or depletion of nonrenewable natural resources
- Minimize the carbon footprint of community housing: construction, operations, and maintenance

Socio-Cultural Domain

- Equitable and affordable access to safe, healthy, and culturally appropriate housing
- Education for sustainability leadership
- Education for behavior and lifestyle changes for energy-efficient living

Technological Domain

- Individual buildings to become net generators of supplied energy; use monitoring technologies
- Districts of residents share supply streams, waste streams, and alternative re-use systems
- Consumer information systems about green technologies, embodied energy, system performance standards, and cost-benefit profiles

Economic Domain

- Life cycle, cost-benefit information systems
- Public/private partnerships for long-term infrastructure to support disaggregated technologies
- Integrated planning for conservation increment financing for carbon-free systems

Public Policy Domain

- Policy Area I. Energy efficiency governance and financial infrastructure
- Policy Area II. Energy performance standards and technology integration
- Policy Area III. Access to energy efficiency and public housing

Regional Infrastructure | Metro Region Interstate Highway Corridor Environs

Environmental Domain

- Green zones
- Landscape plans/corridor
- Landscape plans/interchanges

Socio-Cultural Domain

- Public art
- Information systems
- State blueprint

Technological Domain

- Multi-modal transportation
- Uniform signage
- Wi-Fi access

Economic Domain

- Development tax
- Interchange development plans
- Development councils

Public Policy Domain

- Economic statutes
- Overlay zones
- No-build zones

Key considerations when selecting indicators

Environmental

- Number of miles of zoned/protected edges along the corridor; protect a 500-yard green zone on either side of the corridor
- Corridor landscape plan/identify miles of implementation
- Landscape plans for each interchange along the corridor and number of interchanges with implemented plans

Socio-Cultural

- Centennial public art projects extended along corridor at rest stops and interchanges
- Coordinated exhibits and information systems at rest stops
- Nebraska Blueprint information system: "Visions for Nebraska."

Technological

- Multimodal transportation systems through corridor
- Uniform sign system that designates places and communities of interest
- Wi-Fi and alternative energy technologies along corridor

Economic

- Transportation/consumer tax on businesses and development within two miles of each side of corridor/interchanges
- Interchange development plans required for new and existing interchanges; plans to be based on cost sharing between public and private interests
- Economic planning and development councils along corridor (i.e., connected community markets) with municipal, county, stakeholder representatives whose interests are within 10 miles of each side of corridor

Public Policy

- Statutes to enable the above economic conditions
- Standard system of corridor overlay zones for all present and future interchanges and two miles wide along each side of the interstate corridor
- No-build green space at a minimum width of 500 yards along each side of the corridor and around exits

Regional Growth Management | Communities in the Path of Regional Growth

Environmental Domain
- Environmental assets
- No-build zones
- Green spaces

Socio-Cultural Domain
- Heritage facilities
- Ashland's vision
- Mixed uses plan

Technological Domain
- Wi-Fi access
- Alternative energy systems
- Multi-modal transportation

Economic Domain
- Economic development coalition
- Economic development incentives
- Urban village

Public Policy Domain
- Sub-area plan
- Cross-jurisdictional alliances
- Green protections

Key considerations when selecting indicators

Environmental
- Survey of all environmental assets
- Environmental assets/natural resources designated for protection. No-build zones designated
- Enhance greenness through new green spaces, streetscapes, and public recreation facilities

Socio-Cultural

- Heritage/history sustainable and publicly accessible
- Community-wide vision of the community's future
- Development principles that will enhance the mixed-use, walkable, bikeable character of an urban village

Technological

- Wi-Fi facilities to cover the entire community
- New incentives/installations for alternative energy
- Ashland connected to region via multi-modal transit systems

Economic

- Community economic development coalition enhanced with sustainable principles and strategies for administering from the perspective of the five domains
- Package of public funded incentives to encourage developers to follow the community's development plan
- Specific strategy of economic assistance for the development of affordable housing, urban village lifestyle, mixed uses, and locally owned businesses

Public Policy

- Comprehensive plan revised to include new sub-area plans for development projects and add new protections for land, water, energy, materials, and locally produced food systems
- Cross-county, cross-jurisdictional alliances to provide mutually beneficial and smart growth patterns of land uses, especially at portals to the I-80 corridor.
- Codes and ordinances to support green construction and development on all new building

Conservation Community | Suburban

Environmental Domain
- Environmental survey
- Village plan
- No-build zones

Socio-Cultural Domain
- Food marketing
- Community food plan
- Citizen support

Technological Domain
- Low-tech methods
- Wi-Fi access
- Multi-modal transportation

Economic Domain
- Rural/urban links
- Local ownerships
- Microeconomic cooperatives

Public Policy Domain
- Sub-area plan
- Services plan
- Development incentives

Key considerations when selecting indicators

Environmental
- Site survey of one square mile of existing farmland for natural vegetation, landforms, waterways, and resources; designate no-build or conservation easements as environmental requirements
- Plans for balancing conservation strategies, mixed-use village-style clustered housing, organic farming land uses
- Existing trees, stream banks, watersheds kept in natural state

Socio-Cultural

- Programs with local or regional communities and markets to connect consumers with local food and production
- Community and farming community linked in suburban and rural coalitions, producers/markets, community assisted agriculture
- Common community of citizens working to conserve land, water, energy materials, and food systems

Technological

- Sustainable, appropriate or low-tech methods used for farming, design of community; integrate existing farm structures.
- Wi-Fi wireless electronics throughout the community
- Multi-modal transportation connections to the region

Economic

- Food production system linked to local metro markets in the restaurant, food stores, institutional, and residential sectors
- Village-style housing development arranged with daily needs commercial shops that are locally owned and operated
- Microeconomic cooperatives organized among residents

Public Policy

- Conservation plan and covenants for the community added as a sub-area plan to the county comprehensive plan.
- Appropriate sustainable and affordable relationships determined between community and county for service needs and account for advantages of green design, planning, and development
- Conservation development incentives within the county government (e.g., tax increment financing)

Urban Districts | Near Center Urban Core Neighborhood

Environmental Domain

- Green spaces
- Walkability/bikeability
- District identity

Socio-Cultural Domain

- Urban village
- Safe streets
- Public facilities

Technological Domain

- Multi-modal transportation
- Wi-Fi access
- District energy system

Economic Domain

- City incentives
- Affordable housing
- Locally owned businesses

Public Policy Domain

- Sub-area plan
- Green district
- Development coalition

Key considerations when selecting indicators

Environmental

- Green public spaces and streetscapes increased
- Walkability and bikeability enhanced; connectivity to adjacent districts and pedestrian destinations
- Building stock upgraded; district has a distinct identity

Socio-Cultural

- New mixed uses developed; character of an urban village' emphasis on mixed-income housing with daily needs in close proximity
- Safe streets and public places; new civic plaza
- Public facilities and arts corridor emphasized and accommodated

Technological

- Multi-modal transit and transportation plan through the district
- Wi-Fi electronic access available throughout the district
- Feasibility plans for district energy and utilities system

Economic

- City incentives for the development of infill and new development
- Daily needs commercial shops and stores developed in parallel with affordable and low-income housing
- Developments with locally owned businesses have priority

Public Policy

- Sub-area plan for district incorporated by the city planning board and city council into the city's comprehensive plan.
- Overlay plan for the district to be designated green-by-design
- District citizens' development coalition developed with members, including property owners, stakeholders, businesses, institutions, and residences in the district

Urban Core | Mixed-Use Center/Revitalization

Environmental Domain

- Urban landscaping installations
- East and west anchors
- Pedestrian shopping street

Socio-Cultural Domain

- Emphasis to intersecting nodes/greening
- Civic and art facilities
- Civic plaza

Technological Domain

- Wi-Fi access
- Multi-modal transportation
- Automated information center

Economic Domain

- Economic development coalition
- Micro- economic program
- Affordable housing

Public Policy Domain

- Marketplace coalition
- Green by design
- Mixed uses plan

Key considerations when selecting indicators

Environmental

- Continue and enhance Lincoln's urban landscaping installations (i.e., street trees, water features, street furniture, and sidewalk art).
- Design the adjacent street as a pedestrian-friendly, calm traffic shopping street and connect the street, pedestrian experience to the adjacent, intersecting nodes of green spaces

- Anchor the east and west ends of the marketplace with a major public green space

Socio-Cultural

- Visible emphasis to the intersecting arts corridor street, and the intersecting pedestrian mall
- Give visible recognition to the adjacent civic and cultural facilities
- Civic plaza and the surrounding redeveloped facilities to be designed to function as an outdoor downtown living room

Technological

- Wi-Fi technologies showcased up and down the market street
- Multi-modal transit systems along length of downtown P Street (use new strategy for P Street circulation to motivate re-planning of entire circulation system for downtown)
- Electronic news and information system installed on the market street

Economic

- Marketplace economic development coalition formed with chamber of commerce and other related stakeholder organizations
- Low-interest microeconomics program for start up of locally owned businesses (investigate feasibility among local financial institutions)
- Strategic plan for affordable housing

Public Policy

- Marketplace priorities and timelines (identified by coalition of the DAT, the city, the DLA, and representatives of the developers)
- All new development along the market street conforms to new policies
- City plans, ordinances, and zoning laws clearly enable a new, pedestrian-friendly, energy efficient, green marketplace made up of mixed uses, mixed-income residential, and retail/commerce that support the new urban demographics of the future downtown

Shopping Mall Retrofit | Failed Big Box

Environmental Domain
- Convert parking lot
- Walkable district
- Public parks

Socio-Cultural Domain
- Mixed-use mall
- Housing street
- Civic activity center

Technological Domain
- Transit system
- Wi-Fi access
- District energy system

Economic Domain
- Economic development council
- Economic incentives
- Attract regional developer

Public Policy Domain
- Sub-area plan
- Economic incentives
- Urban village plan

Key considerations when selecting indicators

Environmental
- Auto parking lot converted into an eco-friendly environment
- New plan for pedestrian and bike-friendly landscaping for the surrounding district
- Green spaces and water features protected as parks in the district

Socio-Cultural

- Portions of the existing mall redeveloped into community center-type facilities (e.g., daycare, youth recreation, community social rooms, children's museum, branch library)
- Mall surrounded with mixed-income housing; street relationships exist between housing and redesigned mall facades
- Mall rebranded as city's commercial/civic activity center

Technological

- Public transit system with the activity center as a primary station/destination
- Mall district Wi-Fi system
- District alternative energy/utilities system

Economic

- District economic/planning council to oversee the planning and redevelopment of the area
- City incentives packages to encourage redevelopment
- Plans and redevelopment intentions advertised within the adjacent regional market; development teams secured from region

Public Policy

- New sub-area plan for the district/new plan incorporated into the city's comprehensive plan
- Area studied and declared as blighted to enable the use of public funds to augment the development funding
- Zoning maps and city ordinances changed to accommodate an urban village plan for the district

Urban Indicators | Measures of Sustainability

Environmental Domain

- Access to potable water/change in pollution
- Rate of consumption of water
- Percentage of wastewater treated
- Air quality
- Solid waste generated
- Disposal methods for solid waste
- Volume of recycled material
- Housing/buildings destroyed
- Park land per capita and access/trails, greenspace
- Area of farm and open land used for development
- Land use

Socio-cultural Domain

- City population (demographics)
- Rate of growth or decline
- Average household size and woman-headed households
- Affordable housing deficiency or surplus
- AIDS and other infectious diseases
- Number of hospital beds and medical staff
- Child mortality rates
- Welfare and unemployment rates
- School classrooms at the edges vs. the center
- Crime rates
- Ethnic populations, locations, neighborhoods
- Housing density patterns
- Markets, volume of sales for regionally produced food

Technological Domain

- Energy sources
- Energy consumption rates
- Miles of roadway, type, surface, maintenance cycles

- Public modes of transportation
- Travel time and distance to employment
- Automobile ownership and annual sales
- Miles per ton of food and household essentials (energy)
- Household infrastructure connection levels
- Volume of recycled construction material used
- Digital connections and public access
- Airline transportation and passenger service

Economic Domain
- Household formation rate
- Income distribution
- City product per person
- Local vs. absentee business ownership
- Households below poverty line and median income
- Informal employment
- Urban and regional GDP
- Tax rates
- Public expenditures; infrastructure, services
- Imports and exports
- Regional, national, international trading networks and value

Public Policy Domain
- Economic development
- Distribution of public funds/equity
- Public indebtedness; debt service budgeting
- Health, safety, and welfare expenditures
- Growth management
- Environmental protection
- Transparent government
- Civic leadership development
- Public/private partnerships
- Use of sustainability indicators
- Visioning process; participatory planning

References

1   World Commission on Environment and Development (WCED), 1987. *"Our Common Future,"* New York: Oxford University Press.

2   Joslyn Castle Institute for Sustainable Communities, 2004, *"Flatwater Report,"* www.ecospheres.com/flatwater_metroplex_final2004.pdf.

3   Steward, W. Cecil and Kuska, Sharon B., Ph.D., 2009, UNECE paper, abstract

4   WCED, op. cit.

5   Wheatley, Margaret and Kellner-Rogers, Myron, June 1999, *Journal for Strategic Performance Measurement*, "What Do We Measure and Why? Questions About the Uses of Measurement."

6   ibid.

7   Frisch, Ragnar, 1933, *Econometrica*, Wikipedia, "Econometrics"

8   Hesketh, Therese, Ph.D., Li Lu, M.D., and Zhu Wei Xing, M.P.H., Sept. 15, 2005, *New England Journal of Medicine*, "The Effect of China's One-Child Family Policy after 25 Years."

9   Leichenko, Robin M. and Solecki, William D., Aug., 2008, *Journal for Society and Natural Resources*, "Consumption, Inequity, and Environmental Justice: The Making of New Metropolitan Landscapes in Developing Countries."

10   American Society of Landscape Architects, Jan. 21, 2010, www.asladirt, "The New Green Economy (Part 2): What Does a Sustainable Economy Look Like?"

11   Hawken, Paul, 1983, *The Next Economy*, New York, Holt, Reinhart and Winston.

12   Brown, Lester R., 2006, *Plan B 2.0*, New York, London, W.W. Norton & Company.

13   Slade, Giles, 2006, *Made to Break: Technology and Obsolescence in America.* Cambridge, Mass.: Harvard UP.

14   "Plastic Pollution: Save Our Shores." Save Our Shores: Caring for the Marine Environment Through Ocean Awareness, Advocacy, and Citizen Action. Web. Feb. 27, 2010. www.saveourshores.org/current-projects/plastic-pollution.

15   "Find Recycling Centers and Learn How To Recycle. Web. Feb. 27, 2010. earth911.com.

16   ibid.

17   U.S. Environmental Protection Agency. Web. Feb. 27, 2010. www.epa.gov.

18   McLaren, Carrie. "Are Consumer Products Made to Break? An Interview with Author Giles Slade." Web log post. Stay Free! Daily. 2006. Web. Feb. 25, 2010. blog. stayfreemagazine.org/2007/04/are_consumer_pr.html.

19   "The Story of Stuff." Web. Feb. 26, 2010. www.storyofstuff.com/facts.php.

20   "Sustainability Is Sexy: The Environmental Problem with Coffee Cups." Sustainability Is Sexy - Promoting Sustainable Coffee Cup Use. Web. Feb. 26, 2010. www. sustainabilityissexy.com/facts.html.

21   ibid.

22   ibid.

23   ibid.

24   Slade, op. cit.

25   Tamminen, Terry. "Made to Break Reveals the Roots of Our Throwaway Culture." Grist. June 29, 2006. Web. Feb. 26, 2010.

26   Sustainability Is Sexy, op.cit.

27   Sustainability Is Sexy, op. cit.

28   Twitchell, James B., 1996, *AdCult USA: The Triumph of Advertising in the American Culture*, Columbia University Press, N.Y.

29   Wikipedia The Free Encyclopedia. Wikimedia Foundation, Inc. Web. Feb. 26, 2010. en.wikipedia.org/wiki/Planned_obsolescenc>.

30   ibid.

31   Fooducate, Oct. 25, 2008, "1862 – 2009: A Brief History of Food and Nutrition Labeling," www.fooducate.com

32   U.S. Green Building Council, 1993, Washington, D.C., "Leadership in Energy and Environmental Design (LEED) Rating System for Buildings," 1994.

33   Agenda 21, 1992, United Nations Conference on Environment and Development (Earth Summit), Rio de Janeiro.

34   The Johannesburg Plan of Implementation (Earth Summit 2002), 2002, Johannesburg, South Africa, "UN Millennium Development Goals (MDG)".

35   The Worldwatch Institute, 2004. *State of the World: The Consumer Society*, New York, London, W.W. Norton & Company

36 UNDP

37 American Institute of Architects, 2007, "Municipal Green Building Programs," American Institute of Architects, Washington, D.C.

38 Scottsdale, Ariz., Green Building Program, www.scottsdaleaz.gov/greenbuilding

39 Kofi Annan, 2006, Secretary General, United Nations (1997-2006).

40 Ferdig, Mary, 2008 – 2010, "Nebraska Sustainability Leadership Workshops", Sustainability Leadership Institute and the Joslyn Institute for Sustainable Communties, Omaha and Lincoln, Neb.

41 Doll, Christopher, 2010, "The Population Paradox: Consumption is the Bigger, Fairer Issue," *Our World 2.0*, United Nations University, Tokyo, Japan

42 The Worldwatch Institute, 2007, *State of the World: Our Urban Future*, New York, London, W.W. Norton & Co.

43 U.N. Habitat, 2009, "World Urban Campaign," Citizens Network for Sustainable Development, www.citinet.org.

44 Steward, W. Cecil, and Kuska, Sharon B., published paper, 2007, Passive and Low Energy Architecture Conference (PLEA), National University of Singapore, School of Design and Environment, www.ecosphere.com

45 Meeting of the Minds, 2007, University of California, Berkeley

46 Steward, Kuska, PLEA paper, op. cit.

47 World Commision on Environment and Development, 1987, op.cit.

48 Steward, Kuska, PLEA paper, op. cit.

49 Olson, Richard H. and Lyson, Thomas R., editors, 1999, *Under the Blade: The Conversion of Agricultural Landscapes*, Case Study #13, W. Cecil Steward, "Lincoln Nebraska Public Schools System: The Advance Scouts for Urban Sprawl", Westview Press, Boulder, Colo..

50 World Watch Institute, 2007, op. cit.

51 Joslyn Castle Institute for Sustainable Communities, 2003, Omaha, Lincoln, Nebraska, www.ecospheres.com

52 Steward, W. Cecil, and Kuska, Sharon B., published paper, 2008 Creative Cities Conference, Naples, Italy, www.ecospheres.com

53 Dale, Ling and Newman, "Community Vitality: The Role of Community-Level Resilience, Adaptation, and Innovation in Sustainable Development", January, 2010, Web publication

54   JISC, EcoSTEP^SM Tool, 2004, Flatwater Metroplex Report, Omaha, Lincoln, Neb., www.ecospheres.com

55   JISC, Envisioning Regional Design Charrettes, 2006, Omaha, Lincoln, Neb., www.ecospheres.com

56   Steward, Kuska, PLEA paper, op. cit.

57   Steward, Kuska, Creative Cities paper, op. cit.

58   JISC, Nebraska Sustainability Leadership Workshops (NSLW), 2008-2010, various locations, State of Nebraska, www.nslw.org

59   Steward, W. Cecil, 2002, Mayor's International Business Leaders' Advisory Council (IBLAC), Shanghai, China, www.ecospheres.com

60   ibid.

61   ibid.

62   United Nations Development Program (UNDP), 2003, "The Challenge of Slums: Global Report on Human Settlements", New York, NY

63   JISC, Flatwater Metroplex Report, op. cit.

64   U.S. Green Building Council, LEED standards, op. cit.

65   Capra, Fritjof, 2002, *The Hidden Connections: Integrating The Biological, Cognitive, and Social Dimensions Of Life Into A Science Of Sustainability*, Doubleday, New York, N.Y.

66   Yeang, Ken, 1995, *Designing With Nature: The Ecological Basis for Architectural Design*, McGraw-Hill, New York, N.Y.

67   Lowe, Ernest, 2001, "Circular Renewal System," *Eco-Industrial Handbook for Asian Developing Countries*, Asian Development Bank, Manila, Philippines.

68   Portland, Ore., 2010, "Metro Construction Industry Recycling Toolkit," City of Portland, Ore.

69   JISC, EcoStores Nebraska, www.ecostoresnebraska.org

70   Steward, W. Cecil and Kuska, Sharon B., 2009, United Nations European Commission for Economics (UNECE), "Sustainometrics: Measuring Progress Toward, or Regression from Energy Efficiency and Sustainability," Vienna, www.ecospheres.com

71   ibid.

72   Wheatley, op. cit.

About the Authors

W. Cecil Steward is a professor and dean emeritus of the College of Architecture at the University of Nebraska, where he served as dean for 27 years. In 1996, he founded the Joslyn Institute for Sustainable Communities, with offices in Omaha and Lincoln. He currently serves as the president and CEO of the Institute. Steward is a fellow of the American Institute of Architects, a member of the College of Distinguished Professors in the Association of Collegiate Schools of Architecture, and a former national president of the American Institute of Architects.

Sharon Kuska, Ph.D., is a professor and former associate dean in the College of Architecture at the University of Nebraska-Lincoln. Her areas of interest involve architectural structures, sustainable design, and women in design. She received both the W. Cecil Steward and the H. Robert Douglass Distinguished Professorships at UNL. Kuska is past president of the Nebraska Society of Professional Engineers, a member of the Design Futures Council Executive Board, and vice president of the Joslyn Institute for Sustainable Communities. She is a professional engineer and a LEED Accredited Professional.